Egg, bacon, sausage, chips & beans.... 4.65
Egg, bacon, 2 sausages & chips...........4.30
Egg, bacon, tom's & mushrooms........4.10
Two Eggs, bacon & sausage...............4.10
Egg, bacon, tom's & chips................4.10
Black pudding, egg, chips & beans......3.90
Egg, sausage, tom's & chips...............3.60
Egg, bacon & chips............................3.40
Two sausages & chips........................3.40
Egg, sausage & chips........................3.40
Two Eggs & chips.............................

Baked Bean...................................on 1 to
Fried egg...................................on 1 toa
Scrambled egg............................on 1 toa
Poached egg...............................on 1 toa
Tomatoes griddled.........on 1 to
Mushrooms griddled......on 1 to
Cheese melted ....on 1 to
Bacon griddled.............on 1 to
Sardines & onions.........on 1 to
2 fried eggs..........on 2 to
Extras:........from:....0.70,

Combination of your choice welcome

OMELETTES

corn omelette & chi...
ette & chips...
... & chi...
omelette & ...
omelette & c...
Onion omele...
tte (3 eggs)...
With salad...

Spanish omelette & chips ....
...omelette & chips...........
...om omelette & chips...........
...melette & chips...........
...beef omelette & chips...........8.50.   Extra
...combination of your choice
...hips – ½ salad 70p

O S

(mayonnaise)
(horseradish)
): 4.65, (toma
Special
a baked

EGG BACON CHIPS & BEANS

MORNING
COFFEE

EGG BACON CHIPS & BEANS

50 GREAT CAFES AND THE STUFF
THAT MAKES THEM GREAT

BY RUSSELL M. DAVIES

About the author

RUSSELL M. DAVIES first discovered a taste for fried food while touring the country in a Transit Van, trying to be a pop star. But stardom didn't beckon so he tried writing jokes for the BBC. And that didn't work either, so he's spent the last 15 years working in advertising.

Egg Bacon Chips & Beans started life as a website, won a Yahoo! award as site of the year and became a small phenomenon. This book is Russell's first attempt to build a writing career around his private passions; forthcoming titles include; 'Watching A Lot Of Telly', 'Taking Pictures of Unremarkable Things' and 'Driving Up The M1 With My Family'.

About the cafes

THIS BOOK IS about 50 great cafes, not the 50 best cafes. It's not a contest, it's a celebration and a personal selection. So if I've missed your favourite, it's not a snub, just contact me at www.eggbaconchipsandbeans.com and we'll let the world know.

And actually there's more than 50. Besides the 50 cafe entries there are also lovely pictures of Raffles in Paddington, The River Cafe near Putney Bridge, The Horseshoe on the A90 and Bertorelli's in Newbiggin By The Sea. They are all absolutely magnificent places, we just couldn't quite squeeze them in.

It's also worth noting that great cafes die every day; it's part of the bittersweet life of the cafe lover. Every place in here is extant at the time of writing. But you never know how long they'll last, so support your local cafe before it becomes a mobile phone shop.

And I must extend my huge and sincere thanks to all the owners, staff and customers of the cafes featured in here. You are all heroes.

All the pictures were taken by Russell Davies, Russell Duncan and Tony Lyons. The especially good ones were taken by Russell Duncan, particularly the very nice one on the cover, which was taken at The Shepherdess.

WHY THE EBC&B?

FOR A FEW weeks in the late 1960s the most glamorous place in Britain was Leicester Forest East service station, a newly constructed part of Harold Wilson's white-hot technological revolution. The restaurant interiors were designed by the achingly fashionable Terrence Conran.

It wasn't as cool by the mid-80s when I started going there.

I was having my year off between school and college. Though I had very little intention of going to college, I'd signed on to the enterprise allowance scheme and my plan was to be a pop star. So I was living at home with Mum and Dad. Playing the occasional gig with the band (Whizz For Atoms) and going to lots of practices. This generally added up to a lot of lying in, very late, and a lot of going to bed, very late.

The only place in the entire East Midlands open at these unsociable hours was Leicester Forest East.

I'd sit. Watch the traffic go by. Pretend to be a tragically romantic figure by reading a difficult book. And I'd order one of their standard set breakfasts. Egg, bacon, chips and beans.

And gradually, without me noticing, egg, bacon, chips and beans became my order. It became part of my identity. (A small part, I'm not a nutter.) It became part of how I dwelt on the land (to get all Hopi Indian about it).

Which brings me closer to the reason for this book.

There's nothing more nourishing and affirming than a good fry-up. It fills you up in so many ways. It fills your nose with that irresistible bacon aroma. It fills your plate with an overflowing of bounty (no plate can really hold a decent fry-up). Clearly it's good, honest, down-to-earth food. Nothing fancy here. But there's depth and nuance to this stuff; no chip is quite like another chip, never the same combination of crunchy and smooth, no two eggs are ever fried in precisely the same way, different amounts of crispy burntness, different whites, different yellows, beans are never just beans, bacon, well, what can you say about bacon? Bacon is the uber-food, the uhr-food, bacon is the alpha and omega, bacon is quite nice, bacon is proof of the existence of God.

A great cafe, meanwhile, makes you think and ponder and imagine. You sit in the cafe and dream idle little dreams and think flighty little thoughts. You speculate and postulate and sooner or later you think maybe you'd like to start recording some of these thoughts.

So, sometime in the early 21st century I wrote my first entry on my website: eggbaconchipsandbeans.com. It was some pictures of the Blandford Cafe in London and some little comments.

I felt that some great cafes weren't getting the attention they deserved. Pop culture had gone all foody and pretentious and everyday food and the people who made it were being ignored. And there's something very, definitively, British about the cafe experience.

Like so many of the voyages on which I've embarked, this should have just fizzled out pathetically once I got bored.

But it didn't. And I began to get decent amounts of web traffic (not huge amounts, it's not pornography, but it did OK).

People began visiting the site and posting nice comments and recommending places I should visit. I'd stumbled onto a culture that people had real affection for. The amount of comments I got from outside the UK suggested it was something that made people homesick and nostalgic.

And then I won a prize from Yahoo! (the website people who love exclamation marks). They'd voted the site one of the top ten in the country and a flurry of press articles couldn't resist leading with large pictures of fried food from the website and I suddenly got tons and tons of traffic, including quite a few publishers, and I got the chance to write a book.

Notes: I set myself a few rules for the project. Just to make the thing more interesting and give it that self-satisfied ring of performance art.

Rule One: I'm only going to write about cafes I really like. Every cafe in this book is really good. It's easy to be funny about crap things but there are enough crap books about crap things around and I didn't want to contribute to the crappy Christmas tidal wave.

So this is, obviously, not a definitive list of good cafes. There are loads of other good cafes out there. Equally there are a lot of bad cafes out there. But you'll have to find them for yourselves. And if you find a

THE EBC&B MAP OF BRITAIN

This map might help explain the geography of *Egg Bacon Chips & Beans*, and why so many bits of Britain, with probably excellent cafes, are seemingly neglected.

bad cafe I can only apologise and urge you to try and find the good in it; like Timothy Spall in a Tom Cruise film, there's always a moment to celebrate.

Rule Two: It's all a bit sly and surreptitious. The plan here is not to do glossy photography of glamorous interiors. This is not inspiration for your docklands flat. I took most of the pictures myself with a cheap little digital camera, mostly from where I was sitting and eating. If you see a good photo it was almost certainly taken by my mate Russell Duncan. Mine are just pictures of how these places actually are on a

Scotland's nice. Especially this bit.

I'm a big fan of the North-East

The Lake District. Over-rated

Anne's Mum and Dad live here

We go on holiday a lot here

My Mum and Dad live here

We live here

Sorry. Too far

Days out at the seaside

regular day. There were no arc-lights, no stylists, no models. That should be obvious from looking at the pictures.

A major reason for all this surreptitious behaviour is that a lot of people don't like you taking pictures in cafes. Particularly the clientele. A lot of people have probably assumed I'm from the Dept. Of Work And Pensions or the Child Support Agency or some kind of UFO investigation squad.

Rule Three: Don't get too obsessive about it. They're only cafes. I seldom went out of my way to find these places. They were places that just came along as I lived my life. Consequently you'll probably see evidence of my life in the pictures. You'll see the egg and chips my lovely wife Anne often orders. Or the Star Wars and Playmobil characters my son Arthur often brings with him.

The only exceptions to this 'find them where you find them' rule were two big trips I made to look for cafes that were a little beyond London and the East Midlands. Two big road trips involving many cafes in a few days. I can recommend it.

Rule Four: Don't talk about Fight Club.

Rule Five: There is no Rule Five. There's no Rule Four really, that was just a joke. There are only three rules.

So that's it. Intro over. On with the book.

A Note On Nomenclature

'Café' is just too fancy. Cafes are already over-burdened with spelling requirements so it seems unfair to throw an accent in there as well. And it takes the whole thing just a little too far upmarket; a good cafe is too unpretentious for an accent.

'Caff', though, is going to far the other way. It smacks too much of slumming it, of class tourism, it sounds like a bit like rugby players getting into 'footie'. I think it's occasionally acceptable to say it, but it's demeaning to cafe-owners to write it all the time.

'Cafe' is just right. It's how you normally see the word written. It feels right to give them the credit of that final syllable, but it seems proper and British to drop the accent.

THE LIST OF CAFES

LET'S GO TO WORK. ON AN EGG.

FOR YEARS AND years I never had breakfast. It probably started at college where I spent most of my time in bed and was never up in time for breakfast. And then, starting work, I was always too miserable in the morning to eat anything. So for years and years I never had breakfast.

And my life was as an aching void.

Then, a few years back during one of those periodic bursts of must-change-my-lifeness that everyone gets I decided I had to have breakfast. I'd read in a book it was a good idea. So, being lazy and against cooking, I turned to the cafes of old London town to sate my breakfast appetites.

And my life was as a joyful noise.

I discovered the truth and power of that old 'go to work on an egg' slogan. A truth and power which would only have been enhanced if whoever wrote it could have made something pithy out of 'go to work on an egg, with some bacon, chips and beans'.

A cafe breakfast sets you up incredibly well for the day ahead. It's not just the truckload of calories; it's the space you carve out for planning and thinking and being yourself. As a Californian might say; it's a good time to 'take a deep swim in Lake You'. And we need that me-time when so much of everyone-else-time is crowded with impossible decisions about work-life balance.

This all points to an important conceptual leap you have to make if you're going to embrace the ebcb and 'live your life the ebcb way' (soon to be a major series of advisory pamphlets). You have to start thinking about fry-ups differently.

To some people a fry-up is just a cheap meal, grabbed quickly, unregarded.

To we few but happy EBC&B samurai it's something else. It's a spiritual sanctuary, it's a planning session akin to Churchill's gatherings in the war-room, it's the Algonquin Round Table, even if you're there on your own. It's a time to make elaborate romantic plans or deduce things from articles in the paper. It's the calm before the storm, the pre-match meal, the screw your courage to the sticking place thingy. It's the place and the time where your life finds its centre, its meaning, its purpose and its vision.

And then you go to work.

1

ENDLESS VARIETY

BAR BRUNO / WARDOUR STREET, W1

Bar Bruno is a magnificent sandwich bar/café right in the heart of Soho, which means you get an interesting, mixed crowd; tourists, TV and film people, office workers, builders, taxi-drivers and people pretending to be writers. I was passing one morning and couldn't resist popping in to try out the EBC&B. And I saw, and it was good. Crispy little chips and a textbook egg. Formidable! A big pile of bacon and a mass of beans with a splendid smear of juice up the side of the plate. And all piping hot.

1. It's a magnificent place. Tardis-like. Splendid location. Great graphics. And there's always a full complement of old blokes behind the counter. More than seems strictly necessary. Which guarantees high quality banter at all times of the day and night.

2. A minimalist condiment approach. Anything else you need, I guess you have to ask for it.

4. These green leathery seats are superb – they lend a little note of luxury. And some of them are tiny, just enough for two people opposite each other. Which is perfect for solo newspaper reading.

3. I'm a big fan of the high-up menu board. I love to watch people coming in unsure of what they want. They have to peer up at the board, realise they can't really read it and order something in a panic as it dawns on them that they're keeping everyone waiting. This is another reason I like the EBC&B. If you always have the same thing you get none of this analysis paralysis; you're straight in there with the illusion of certainty.

Breakfasts (Served all Day)	
Egg & Bacon	250
Egg, Bacon & Sausage	300
Egg, Bacon & Tomatoes	300
Egg, Bacon & Bubble & Squeak	340
2 Sausages, Chips & Beans	320
Sausage, Egg & Chips	250
2 Fried Eggs on 2 Toast	2.00
2 Scrambled Eggs on 2 Toast	2.00

CAFE D'JACONELLI / 570 MARYHILL ROAD, GLASGOW

This brilliant place was used as a location in *Trainspotting*, (it's the scene just before Spud's interview, but they make the cafe look quite seedy, and it's not seedy – it's magnificent). It's a perfect example of the traditional Italian/Scottish combination of fried food and ice-cream.

There's this perfect engraving/etching thing on the door – with a brilliant design that shows you a huge ice-cream with an ashtray and cigarette next to it. The Scots know what's good for them. Fry-ups. Ice-cream. Fags.

It's just gorgeous. The deep red leather. The fish tank. That beautiful lamp.

3. Lovely egg. Lovely bacon. Lovely chips. Lovely beans. Lovely.

4. All the necessary condiments. Right there. Ready to go. And all high-quality – Heinz and HP.

Look at those piles of sliced bread packets, all ready to go in the glass cabinet by the counter. That's going to feed an army of office workers and taxi drivers.

BLANDFORDS / CHILTERN STREET, W1

Blandfords was the first place I visited when I embarked on this project. Though I didn't know I was embarking on anything at the time. I just happened to have my camera with me and when I got home I thought I'd stick it up on the website. And a few months later there was a ton of cafes and a few months after that there's a book. Blandfords was the inspiration because it's a simple unassuming place that does reasonable food at reasonable prices and that's something that's not been celebrated enough. And that's what inspired the whole bally process.

1. The chips were lovely; a hint of crunchiness and a hint of browning. Nice sauce, nice bit of bacon too, though not a ton of it. The beans were slightly exotic. I'm not convinced they were a leading brand but I could have been wrong.

2. When I looked at all these pictures again, I noticed that though there's a lot of people in them, they're all blokes. That's a pattern that recurred during my cafe travels.

3. A very nice drop of tea. But it never seems quite right to drink tea from a cup branded with a coffee logo. I always wonder about the economics of cups like this. Do you think they get them for free? Or just reduced?

4. I remember there being a signed photo of Ray Davies of The Kinks on the wall, which further enhanced that air of splendidly faded English glory.

EUSTON SANDWICH BAR / EUSTON ROAD, NW1

The Euston Sandwich Bar is a marvellous place on the North side of the Euston Road, it's tiny but always bustling and friendly. And it always offers a welcoming glow in the bleak office/industrial landscape of the Euston Road.
The EBC&B is faultless – look at the aesthetics, nicely reduced beans, those modern crunchy chips that really absorb the bean juice, and a beautiful pale egg. And the bacon is hugely flavourful – it tastes fresh off the pig.

1. The signs are great. Really classic and clean – again a welcome contrast to the corporate wasteland around there.

2. See the seats? That's how to run a well-ordered cafe.

3. I didn't get great photos inside, I was stuck round the corner, but it's got great tables and counters and those magnificent orange plastic seats bolted to metal frames. You can't have customers moving themselves around when you've not got a lot of space.

At lunchtime there are huge queues of people getting a sandwich to take back to their desk. But you can always find a seat, even if you have to sit next to someone else. Anne and I were sitting there one day, sat next to a bloke chatting on his mobile earpiece thing about this gruesome operation he was about to have.

The perfect cafe experience.

4. Simple condiment display. And isn't that the best sugar dispenser? I can't be doing with those spouty ones. They don't give you enough control.

5. Lovely tables. Lovely white crockery.

GAMBARDELLA'S / 48 VANBURGH PARK, SE3

A while back, as I was heading South East to visit the dinosaurs of Crystal Palace, this seemed like the perfect place for lunch. And I have to say it's one of the friendliest places I've ever been. Really lovely people. Just look at that fridge. Perfect. You feel you could get the fond-remembered ice-cream of your childhood from there.

1. The interior is magnificent. All polished and ancient and shiny. All set off by modern accoutrements like a high-viz jacket.

2. The EBC&B was lovely too. Mammoth chips (which are apparently much healthier), discreet egg, generous beans and a nice bit of bacon. This is what I'd call a pensioner-style EBC&B. Nothing show-offy. A reasonable size and good value. Which is good because there seem to be a lot of pensioners who make this a regular destination. Especially in the smoking half of the building – which is the lovely authentic bit.

EAT LIKE A QUEEN FOR £3

1. You can also eat like a king if you'd prefer.

2. A helpful photographic menu accompanied by charming illustrations of Mr Egg himself.

MR EGG / 22 HURST STREET, BIRMINGHAM

Mr Egg is a glorious place in the middle of Birmingham. The interior is great practical cafe stuff. Easy to clean. Suitable for all kinds of patrons; the drunk and the sober. But it's also got some great little hints of exuberant individuality.

3. The EBC&B is splendid. Look at that decorative plate for a start. The chips are crisp and delicate, the beans juicy and energetic and the bacon's got that delicious hint of carbonisation. And bless that modest little egg, hiding away at the back there.

4. The coup de cafe – a large cloth egg stapled to the ceiling.

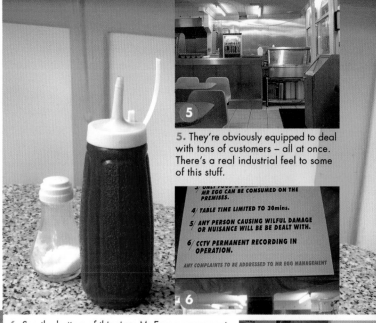

5. They're obviously equipped to deal with tons of customers – all at once. There's a real industrial feel to some of this stuff.

> ... ONLY FOOD ...
> MR EGG CAN BE CONSUMED ON THE PREMISES.
> 4/ TABLE TIME LIMITED TO 30mins.
> 5/ ANY PERSON CAUSING WILFUL DAMAGE OR NUISANCE WILL BE BE DEALT WITH.
> 6/ CCTV PERMANENT RECORDING IN OPERATION.
> ANY COMPLAINTS TO BE ADDRESSED TO MR EGG MANAGEMENT

6. See the bottom of this sign: Mr Egg management. Simultaneously sinister and cute. Like the Mafia in Toy Town, running a speakeasy around the back of Noddy's place.

7. Sugar is one of those difficult decisions cafes have to make. Will it be sachets, bowls or dispensers? Or will it be – as per Mr Egg – one of these fantastic sugar stations? With, in this instance, a place for the dumping of tea bags. Mr Egg's gone for the plastic spoons but I'm always a fan of the places that have just a few metal spoons – stored in a mug of lukewarm water for extra hygiene.

THE OLD SMITHY / (B5055) MONYASH, DERBYSHIRE

This is The Old Smithy at Monyash. Heart of the Peak District. Not far from Lathkill Dale. It's a tiny place but it does a magnificent EBC&B. And muddy boots are welcome.

1. This is proper food. I'm often not that bothered about ingredients and all that – it's not necessarily the important bit of a fry-up. But this is high-quality stuff. You get the feeling this pig was hiking around the dales only 5 minutes ago. And the chips and everything else are delicious.

2. But they're not resting on their laurels. There's a nice new extension around the back, a little extra room for when they get busy. This is where we sat.

3. Half of the place is this magnificent old room, covered in musical instruments and odd paraphenalia. It feels like a powerful node in the Peak District walking/folk music/real ale matrix. A splendid place.

4. A fry-up in the winter and ice-cream in the summer. That's the British countryside experience.

5. You want a perfect day? Get up early, make yourself a flask of tea, take a long walk through Lathkill Dale, pausing to sample your flask at a little footbridge. Then head to the Old Smithy for a high quality breakfast.

PELLICCI'S / BETHNAL GREEN ROAD, E2

Pellicci's is an East End institution which has fed gangsters and civilians, poor and posh, traders and tourists. It's very friendly and slightly scary; warm, worn, ancient and modern. And it's one of the few 'classic cafes' that's not really under threat. Firstly, it's not the most in demand property in the world around there. Secondly, the place has recently received Grade II Listed status. The listing inspectors said Pellicci's had a 'stylish shop front of custard Vitrolite panels, steel frame and lettering as well as a rich Deco-style marquetry panelled interior, altogether representing an architecturally strong and increasingly rare example of the intact and stylish Italian caf that flourished in London in the inter-war years'. Which is nice. And so they get all sorts of visitors. Architecture students, design aficionados and tourists attracted by Pellicci's role in the Kray Brothers' legend. But the most important thing is, of course, the grub.

1. And it's top nosh. Big, fat satisfying chips. Flavourful bacon. Piping beans. A strangely compelling egg. And that wooden handle on the knife gives you that little note of quality.

2. I like the condiment cluster. It's all about verticals. Long thin shapes. And the sauce hues somehow match the tonal values of the cafe. Ooh, hark, at me; I've come over all Linda from *Changing Rooms*.

3. The atmosphere is dense with history and fat. A lot's happened here. And a lot of food has been fried and eaten.

PETE'S EATS / 40 HIGH STREET, LLANBERIS, GWYNEDD

Pete's is a brilliant mountaineers' and walkers' cafe in Llanberis, which also delivers huge, steaming plates of high-quality food to ordinary tourists like you and me. It's a huge generous place with a charming ethos and character to it. It's a cafe that demonstrates the true strength of the British lies in our nutterdom; in our embrace of peculiar passions and our celebration of the eccentric.

1. The EBC&B is appropriately mountainous. Piles of great stuff mounded together like the cook has been watching *Close Encounters* recently. The chips were particularly special; all kinds of different shapes and textures like shards of shale or something. (Shall I stop with the mountaineering analogies now?)

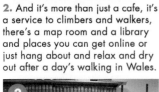

4. The condiments are big too.

5. Pete's wears its heart on its sleeve. There are pictures of climbing and climbers all over the place.

RHYNGRWYD — INTERNET
LLYFRGELL MAP — MAP LIBRARY
LOLFA — LOUNGE AREA
GWYBODAETH — INFORMATION

2. And it's more than just a cafe, it's a service to climbers and walkers, there's a map room and a library and places you can get online or just hang about and relax and dry out after a day's walking in Wales.

3. You can always tell the vigour of a cafe from the number and the up-to-dateness of the posters and notices.

Look at these two fellows. Best condiments ever.

TONY'S / NORTHCOTE ROAD, SW11

Tony's is a bastion of ungentrification in Battersea's Nappy Valley – fuelled by the appetites of the stall-holders on the market.

2. A great EBC&B. Fascinating texture to the egg. Like it's been cooked at least a couple of different ways. Some of them previously unknown to culinary science. Very respectable amount of bacon and irresistible chips.

3. The interior is redolent of all sorts of Battersea nostalgia; 60s *Up The Junction*-type black and white gloom. Or the 1979 Squeeze version. A splendid place.

THE CHICKEN IS INVOLVED, THE PIG IS COMMITTED

DURING THE RUN-UP to the first Gulf War ('the gulf war to end all gulf wars') General Norman Schwarzkopf was apparently asked what he meant by saying that US forces were 'involved but not committed.' He replied that if you think about a nice plate of bacon and egg then the chicken is involved, but the pig is committed.

I like that notion. And I think it's as true of this book as it is of Gulf War analogies. Lots of pigs have been harmed in the manufacture of this book. But the worst that's happened to chickens is all the horrible stuff that free range people tell you they don't do. And that's why bacon is preceding eggs in this book – if not in its title.

Bacon drives vegetarians mad. It's the food they always go on about. It's the thing that finally breaks them. Why? Because it's absolutely bloody delicious. And it's not a vegetable. So ha! to all you vegetarians. Your choice may be ethically and nutritionally admirable, but it's tastually inferior.

A poll conducted by Danepak found that 39% of the British population felt their Monday mornings would be made more cheerful by the inclusion of a bacon roll. And that 37% think a bacon butty improves their mood. And that 17% would rather have a bacon butty everyday than make love everyday. Another poll found that the three most popular smells in the UK are baked bread, bacon and coffee. In that order. So you can see why a bacon roll and a coffee is such a popular choice when people need cheering up. That single simple meal combines the three most popular smells in the country. It doesn't seem much, but think how hard that is to do. If you combine the three most popular colours in the world you just end up with brown. But the three most popular smells – they come together in a taste sensation that staves off depression, can cost less than £2 and gets you through the first unpleasant status meeting of the day.

Could that be why we eat 450,000 tonnes of bacon a year? More than any other country in Europe. That's a lot of bacon. If we wanted to launch all that bacon into space instead we'd need around 65,000 Soyuz rockets or 120,000 space shuttles. And all that bacon costs us £430 million. You could buy a couple of Chelsea footballers with that.

Of course, pigs give us much more than bacon. By which I don't mean they gave us viaducts and the pre-Raphaelites but that so much of a pig is absolutely delicious. Grimond de la Reyniere, who was apparently the very first restaurant critic, put it best when he said 'the pig is an encyclopaedic animal. It is a veritable meal on hooves. One throws away nothing.'

Though we mustn't get too carried away with this sentimental tosh. Baden-Powell really enjoyed the noble sport of pig-sticking, describing is as 'a glorious pursuit, with a good weapon in your hand, of an enemy whom you want to kill.'

That's very much how I think of a lovely piece of well-fried bacon.

Nothing. I've got nothing for N. Nothing. Nil. Nada. Nought.

A COMMON THING, DONE UNCOMMONLY WELL

H.J. HEINZ SAID his aim in life was simply 'to do a common thing uncommonly well'. Isn't that nice? Isn't that a perfect way to look at life? Doesn't that perfectly sum up what a good baked bean is all about? Especially a Heinz baked bean.

Heinz beans are definitely a common thing. They sidle into every aspect of our lives. They're the perfect childhood comfort food. They keep students alive during the long winter months when beer alone doesn't provide sufficient calories. They're the perfect antidote to a cold and dismal afternoon watching your team getting relegated. They're an essential component in any British home. And, of course, they're American.

And Heinz do beans uncommonly well. Let me count the ways:

1. They disguise their vegetable roots with great aplomb. The orange thing in the tin seems so far removed from the idea of 'a bean' that it never crosses children's minds to reject it on vegetable grounds. And it doesn't even taste like a vegetable; it doesn't have that self-satisfied, fibrous crunch. Instead a good baked bean has the yieldy, meaty feel of an incredibly tender steak. And even better, an 80g portion of beans apparently counts as one of the five portions of fruit and vegetables you're supposed to have every day. Add a grilled tomato to your ebcb and you're well on your way to a healthy lifestyle.

2. They're orange. Genius. Who'd have thought of making food orange? (Apart from oranges, obviously, and no one thought of that, that was God. Or evolution. Or both.) Such a rare burst of optimistic colour on the miserable post-war British culinary scene. Grey potatoes, grey meat, grey peas and then open the tin and here comes the orangeness. Marvellous. No wonder everyone fell in love. And no wonder subsequent child-oriented food inventions have tended to be orange. Fish fingers? Why are they orange? It's not because cod are orange – it's because of baked beans. Then they go and do the common thing even more uncommonly well by making the tin that particular bluish colour which makes the beans look even better.

3. You don't have to cook them. How good is that? A food stuff that tastes marvellous when piping hot, but that you can eat perfectly well when stone cold. Out of the tin. With your hands. Lying on the

Formica: is it mined or grown?

kitchen floor because you're too drunk to stand. That's versatile. That's a high quality food stuff.

4. They're personalisable. Every tin of beans is the same. They're consistently delicious. But as soon as they hit the pan the personality of the cook takes over. You can never cook beans badly (see point 3 above) but you can cook them in your own individual way. How much heat? How long? Simmering or blasting? How much juice do you boil off? Do you aim for that gooey bean paste so many people like or do you strive to preserve the individuality of each bean? It's up to you. The bean allows you to really express yourself. To speak of who you are. To be all you can be. To bean all you can bean.

5. They last forever in those neat little tins. They'll survive the collapse of the planet, the melt-down of the sun and the long, slow entropic death of the universe. This is how the world ends; not with a bang but with insectoid apocalypse survivors trying to open a can of beans.

6. They have the best slogan. 'Beanz Meanz Heinz' is the best advertising slogan ever. And was officially recognised as such in 2000 by The Advertising Slogan Hall Of Fame. It's good firstly because it's memorable – it's got that little internal rhyme and that quirky spelling which means it instantly sticks in the head. It's also good because it 'claims the generic'. It doesn't try and tell you that Heinz beans are better in some way, it just says that Heinz beans are the very definition of beans. There is no other sort of beans. If the beans aren't Heinz then they're not really beans. That's clever.

7. They're top secret. Apparently only four people know the secret baked beans recipe. Doesn't that lend them a little note of extra glamour? They're almost quite sexy now you know that.

There's some dispute about who actually wrote 'Beanz Meanz Heinz'. The acknowledged author was Maurice Drake who apparently wrote the line in a pub in 1967, but recently a Mr Jeff Bennet has emerged, claiming he wrote the line 10 years earlier as part of a Heinz competition which netted him a shopping trip to Hamleys. He's not bitter about it though and is keen to dissociate himself from the mis-spelling that Drake came up with. Which of course is most of the genius of the idea. Oh well.

THE EBC&B HANDY BEAN COLOUR CHART

Use The Magic of Beans to Make Exciting Colour Choices For Your Home and Clothes

EBC&B001
Florida Sunset

EBC&B002
Hi-Viz Fizz

EBC&B003
Orangutany

EBC&B004
Jaffa

EBC&B005
Not Quite Heinz

EBC&B006
A Bit Too Hucknall

EBC&B007
Browned Off

EBC&B008
Alien Beanz

EBC&B009
Gingernut

EBC&B010
Unpleasantly Like A Wound

EBC&B011
Pale Imitation

EBC&B012
Rust

Cut out and keep

THE DUALITY OF EGGS

HERE ARE THE two things:

Eggs Are Funny

Eggs are funny food. Throw a brick and it's terrorism. Throw an egg and it's comedy. Burn a book and it's fascism. Burn an egg and it's cookery. (Cabbages were once considered comedy items but since it's become well known that the sound-effects of punches to the head in Raging Bull were created by hitting cabbages they've become more sinister.)

They look funny to start with. Round things are funnier than angular things. (8, for instance, is a funnier number than 4). And eggs are more funny because they're not spherical – they're a bit distorted. They're, well, egg-shaped. They don't roll properly. They topple. They need to go in a cup. They're odd. They're Humpty Dumpty. They're funny.

And the word is funny. Egg. It's just funny to say. Imagine Rowan Atkinson as Edmund Blackadder saying it. Egg. Eggy. Eggbound. It's funny. It's not an obvious comedy word like knob or kipper. It's not slightly sexual. It's funny because of the sound and the image it conjures up.

Eggs Are Boring

For some strange reason eggs attract pedants. They attract the people who are always trying to tell you exactly how things should be done. It's bizarre but true.

Open any cookbook and you'll find they always start with detailed advice on how to cook the 'perfect egg'. They start with the perfect boiled egg, then on to the perfect scrambled egg and then as some point presumably end up with instructions for the perfect coddled egg on a bed of something.

All their methods for attaining perfection demand strict adherence to detailed instructions about boiling duration, freshness of egg, pinches of salt, alignment of stars and menstrual cycles of participants. Sometimes it's three-and-a-half minutes, sometimes it's four. But everything is about finding perfection in something that is, essentially, completely unknowable. An egg is an organic object, not a reagent bottle and

every egg is different; in chemical composition, in the amount it was shaken up and down on the way back from the shops. Yet these pedants insist on striving for perfection. The best example of this vicious egg pedantry is probably the leading bore of the twentieth century; James Bond. Ian Fleming's books are full of detailed descriptions of how Bond liked his eggs: boiled for three-and-a-half minutes, must be brown, must be from French Marans hens, must be very fresh. This just gives you one more reason not to sit next to Bond at a dinner party. If he's not going on about the cars he's driven, the women he's slept with or the gadgets he owns he'll be bending your ear about eggs. Avoid him. And don't ever go into a cafe with him.

EGGS AND THE TYRANNY OF CHOICE

THE GREAT THING about cafes is the limited amount of choice. That's what set breakfasts are for. They narrow your culinary universe into understandable clumps – you look for an acceptable solution to your foody need-state, you don't push for perfection. And everyone's happy.

In fact this is one of the hardships about ordering egg, bacon, chips and beans. Although it has its own mythic origins as a set meal at Leicester Forest East (see intro) it's not often a standard British combination, so ordering it can be a trial.

Typically a request for an ebcb is at first met with a worrying pause as the cafe-representative mentally processes a deviant food request and you wait nervously to see if it's deemed an acceptable order. Then with an almost imperceptible sigh the much chewed biro is dragged across the scrappy paper of the order pad – scrawling something like sausage, eggs and chips. You er and hum incisively and say er no, sorry, actually bacon, please, and chips and beans. Peas? They say. No, beans. OK. Drink? Tea please. Coffee? No, tea. OK. Take a seat.

This should be regarded as a good transaction. All the items are available. There have been no tears, no fighting and not too much embarrassment.

My favourite scenario is always the shoutback. You state your order and the person serving you merely shouts it back to the kitchen and the food arrives a few moments later with nothing ever being written down. Then, when you go and pay, you remind the server what you had and he or she makes up a price to charge you. I love that. It's a kind of post-literate improvised theatre.

SO LET'S GO back to choice. And let's look at the world capital of choice, the Ottoman Empire of options: the average American cafe/diner.

Now, I have to say, I adore these places. They're sumptuous palaces of sustained pleasure. The graphics are always gorgeous, the food is always generous, the people are always lovely. I think those years of watching *Happy Days* after school (and *Saved By The Bell* after work) have conditioned me to appreciate a diner like Pavlov's dogs appreciate Big Ben. If you need proof of my enthusiasm then consider the fact that in the five years I spent in the States I gained three stone, and, ahem, it wasn't all muscle.

Nevertheless I have to admit that the choices they offer you are always terrifying. Then you notice that no one around you seems to be even looking at the menu; they seem to just be deciding what they want to have and then just ordering that.

Almost instantly you have to order a drink and while you're doing it some glasses of water arrive. And you're not sure whether they're someone else's order or what, but you try to ignore that and you order a cup of tea and then you have to choose what kind of tea, because they don't do generic tea like cafes do. Then you have to choose between lemon and tea and milk and then they go away and leave you for a while. Breath. Just breathe.

Then they're back and you order some tasty sounding combination of fried stuff and you think you're OK for a minute. But then, comes the moment of truth – the egg question.

You cannot believe the amount of egg choice you have. Scrambled. Soft-Boiled. Hard-Boiled. Coddled. Fried. Poached. Basted. And of course you can often opt to just have the whites, or demand eggs high in omega 3s or request that the egg be rotated widdershins before a conclave of cardinals while being cooked by the magnified light from Alpha Centauri.

For ages I'd always opt for scrambled because I learned that led to the thing you always want – 'no further questions'. Whereas

In case you're currently stuck in a diner, pondering these questions – here's the run-down:

Over light – the egg white and the yolk are both hot, but still a bit runny. (Hmm. Not sure. Not for me.)

Over easy – the white is almost entirely cooked. The yolk is still a little runny. (Almost there.)

Over medium – the white is completely cooked (and perhaps starting to crinkle at the edges) the yolk still has a hint of runniness. (Perfect. Stop there. That's for me.)

Over well – Both the egg and the yolk are cooked. (Stop. You've gone too far. Go back one.)

By 'over' they mean they've started with a 'sunny-side up' egg, your basic fried egg, and flipped it over once.

opting for fried always led to the question of how you wanted it. And I just didn't know. What's sunny-side up? What's over-easy? Does it make that much difference?

That's why I so love the British cafe. I've ordered a lot of fried eggs in a lot of cafes. And no-one has ever asked me how I'd like that cooked. And as long as it is actually cooked, I'm not bothered how.

WHAT DO YOU EXPECT FOR £4?

EVERY NOW AND then I'll recommend a cafe to someone and they'll come back and complain that the food was no good. Sure it was friendly and clean but actually the quality of the cooking wasn't that high. This always puzzles me. It seems to be missing the point somehow.

What do you expect for £4?

I once got told this hoary old story set in the world of advertising. It's probably told in all kinds of professions, because it's a useful idea, and it definitely applies to cafes.

A client once marched in to see an ad man and demanded that his new ads be done at great speed, at hugely reduced cost and that they be much better than they used to be. The advertising man sighed, drew a triangle on a bit of paper and wrote three words, one at each corner. The words were 'Fast' and 'Good' and 'Cheap'. And he simply said to the client; 'Pick two'.

I realise now that I've written that like a joke with some kind of a punch-line. Sorry if you were expecting a laugh. But instead you've got something much better. You've got a point. And it's a valuable point. You can very rarely get something that's good and fast and cheap. You can have fast and good but not cheap, or good and cheap but not fast, or, well, you can see where this is going.

And that's worth bearing in mind when it comes to cafes. They all tend to offer fast and cheap, so if you get good as well then you're very lucky. Or you're basing your lifestyle on this book because every cafe in here delivers on fast, cheap and good.

(Except for the odd one, like the Old Smithy, that doesn't do dead cheap, but actually does top quality food.)

DIANA'S DINER / ENDELL STREET, WC1

Remember The Beloved? They were an indie band in the mid-80s that suddenly became an acid house success in the late-80s. They did a lovely song called *Sun Rising* that you still hear every now and then. They started in Diana's Diner; after one of them placed the following ad in the music press: 'I am Jon Marsh, founder member of the Beloved. Should you too wish to do something gorgeous, meet me in exactly three years' time at exactly 11am in Diana's Diner, or site thereof, Covent Garden, London, WC2'. I don't know why, but Diana's feels exactly like the right kind of place for that kind of story. It's not the smartest cafe in the world (some would call it slightly tatty, I prefer to think of shabby chic) but it has a really nice vibe. It's a place you'd want in your memories.

1. And the grub is exemplary. Excellent chips and lots of them. Good meaty beans. Nice, chewy bacon.

2. Condiment-wise, all the bases are efficiently covered. No need to reach around to a neighbouring table.

DINO'S GRILL / COMMERCIAL STREET E1

Dino's Grill is just down from Spitalfields Market and Brick Lane and is hence open on a Sunday morning. Which is a boon. It's surprising how few cafes are open early on a Sunday morning, given the general societal requirements for hangover cures and newspaper reading facilities.

2. Classic condiment cluster. Except… where's the brown? I had to hustle to an adjacent table to collect a spare. I like all the shiny metal against the shiny wood effect. Makes everything light and almost space-age.

3. A faultless display of symmetrical ashtray placement.

1. A visually thrilling EBC&B. I was offered a choice of chips and went for 'fat ones' – so I'd be excited to see the thin ones. They must be very thin. I think I caught them slightly on the hop, it was very early in the morning so the bacon and beans were a little undercooked. But I found absolute redemption in the egg. Gold and white like a high-quality medallion resting against a dress shirt. This is what I love about a cafe. The food doesn't have to be perfect for you to have a perfect cafe experience.

4. This is the kind of branding I like on a cup. Local businesses getting their name around. I've always wanted to do this. Just put my picture on a mug with some positive message (Russell is a nice and funny man), just to see if people start to smile at me more.

5. Gorgeous booths.

DOLPHIN RESTAURANT / GREAT DARKGATE STREET, ABERYSTWYTH

This is an interesting and delightful fry-up. The Dolphin is basically a lovely big chip shop so fry-ups aren't really their core activity. But chip shop chips make a really interesting difference. They're fat and delicious like only chip shops can do. The beans are thrown on like Jackson Pollock might have done it. The bacon's delicious. The eggs are perfect. It was a cold day, I'd driven a long way. I don't think I've ever enjoyed a fry-up as much as I did this one.

1. Imagine how exciting and welcoming this neon must be on a wet winter's night.

2. The simplest condiment cluster. It's a chip shop. It's all you really need.

3. The booths are fantastically generous; geared to the holidaying chip-shop patron. You can get a large family in here. And they can be a large-arsed family too. These aren't the anorexic booths of central London. These are booths that let you loosen your belt. I was very grateful for these.

4. I love these two-sided metal shelf/cabinet things. They look like something from a works canteen or a New York deli in a Doris Day film.

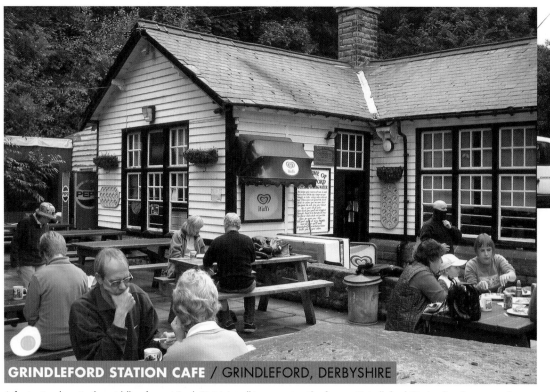

GRINDLEFORD STATION CAFE / GRINDLEFORD, DERBYSHIRE

A fantastic place in the middle of great Peak District walking country, the former Grindleford Station has become a haven for hikers and bikers – the twin bastions of the Peak District economy. With a common interest in large plates of fried food and specially designed waterproof clothing.

1. Great little chips, small, so there's greater proportion of surface area and therefore more friedness. Big, thick bacon and a pale egg. Sauce comes from huge communal/industrial dispensers.

2. They also sell magazines and maps. And everywhere is covered with handwritten signs dealing with some issue or another. Toilets, kids, coach parties, where to take your pots when you're done. The kind of non-friendly friendliness that works around here. Friendliness that depends upon a clear understanding of the rules.

THE HOME OF
GRINDLEFORD
NATURAL SPRING WATER

All the condiment bases are covered, and there's a very classy sugar bowl. Like you're at The Ritz or something. That must have pushed the budget a bit.

LINO'S / ALFRED PLACE, WC1

Lino's is a bit of an institution. A friendly, busy place around the back of Tottenham Court Road – which makes it very handy for building up your strength before you do your electronics shopping. And I like the fact that they persist in calling themselves a snack bar. What is a snack bar these days? Where's the line between a snack and a meal? I don't know and I don't care. But I love snack bars and I love Lino's.

1. Who is he? What's going on here? What's he got on this tray?

2. They do an exemplary EBC&B and deliver it very quickly, almost suspiciously quickly. Like they've got some mind-reading device that knows what you're going to order and starts preparing it before you get there. Lovely hot chips and a very weedy egg, but in a good way.

3. There's something about a booth. A booth is just a better place to eat than a sad isolated table. A table is an island, a booth is a cave. It's welcoming, friendly, comforting. Booths rule. (And I include Cherie in that.)

Who nicked all the flowers?

ORANGERY CAFE / MARKEATON PARK, DERBY

The Markeaton Park cafe sounds very grand. It's in the old orangery of Markeaton Hall, ancestral home of the Mundy family. But Markeaton is no longer that grand. The hall was left to Derby Council in the 20s but after the war they let it slide into wrack and ruin until it was demolished in the 60s. This was my local park when I grew up and it was pretty grim, but, like so many parks it's had a bit of a renaissance recently, and the cafe's part of that. It's not fancy, but it's dead right for a big municipal park.

1. The EBC&B is delumptious (as Roald Dahl might have it). And all the better for being alfresco. I like the way a tributary of beans dribbles towards the egg. Solid chips, very interesting egg, nice thick bacon.

2. It's nice to have a view over your EBC&B. Shame all the flowerbeds were devoid of flowers. When they're in there it all looks lovely.

4. A great cafe has something for everyone.

3. Of course if you really want to you can sit inside. There's a nice, cavernous former orangery for you to sit in but why would you? You're in a park, you should run in, grab your candyfloss and your sherbet dabs and rush outside to feed the ducks, bark your shins and lose a limb in the adventure playground.

THE MARKET PLACE CAFE / MARKET PLACE, OFF OXFORD STREET, W1

The Market Place cafe is one of my favourite ever cafes. I used to work just around the corner from here and I was in here a lot. And it never let me down. It's a gloriously chirpy and welcoming place. It's down some steps in a basement near Oxford Street and there's a sign outside saying it was established in 1938, which, when you think about it, was a great year to start an underground cafe in London.

2. The Marketplace always gives you your tea in these nice teapots and gives you your own little milk jug. I love the little bit of specialness that connotes. And the ability it grants you to self-medicate your milk.

1. Hmmm. I've eaten this a lot. And I've always loved it. Look at that superb bacon and that elegant tranche of beans. The chips are fat and crisp and crunchy. Textbook chips straight from Good Chip U. And the egg is being very modest, around the back there.

3. It may be a basement but the sun streams in when it's nice. And everything seems to be shiny. Shiny fridge, shiny chairs and tables, shiny everything. Shiny, happy people serving food.

4. High quality documents and a high quality menu. Extensive use of desktop publishing and a laminating machine.

OBERTELLI'S EATING HOUSE / LEADENHALL MARKET, EC3

Obertelli's is a splendidly traditional place in the heart of the city. You can imagine it featuring in a film about the 80s – barrow boys turning into traders and staying in touch with their roots through fry-ups at Orbertelli's.

1. They do a very high quality EBC&B. A nice bit of quality bacon and a lovely, luxurious egg, spread out like a sunbather. And a big pile of nice beans. The fries are fry-types – crunchy and crisp. All nicely demarcated with very little overlap.

2. There's less room for eating downstairs, just stools or the tables outside. But upstairs is a land that time forgot. Lots of white tiles and blokes focused on eating. A good, focused atmosphere. Dedicated to the noble art of stuffing your face at a reasonable pace, then leaning back, loosening the belt and pronouncing about the events of the day over a newspaper.

CRISPNESS AND SOFTNESS

CHIPS ARE EXTRAORDINARILY, remarkably delicious. One of the most compelling and bewitching substances known to man. It's such a beautiful thing (and perhaps evidence of the existence of God) that the humble, tedious potato can be transformed, by the simple addition of heat and fat, into this delightful piece of sensory heaven. And that's a mystical process yet to be adequately explained by human science. Let's face it, if fat and heat normally made for bewitching beauty the beaches of Benidorm would be very different places.

This alchemy is all the more magical because the potato is such an unremarkable beast, so easy to overlook. The Spanish first found them in the Andes around 1537 and they had no idea what a versatile, efficient food they'd found. They didn't bring any back to Spain for another 70 years and even then it was probably just a diverting trifle (probably the sixteenth century equivalent of the amusingly shaped vegetables on *That's Life*).

However, you don't need me just telling you that chips are delicious. You know that. What you want is a detailed and rigorous analysis of the role in the chip in the complex culinary-cultural construct that is the ebcb. (Don't you? You don't? Then you're reading the wrong book, pal. Can I perhaps refer you to one of my esteemed colleagues in the 'real books about stuff that matters' section?) So let's think about that for a minute, and let's see if we can squeeze in any torturous analogies with pompous rock ensembles.

Imagine your EBC&B is made up of the members of Queen.

Roger Taylor (the drummer) is your bacon. Essential. Got to have it. Makes a difference if it's bad but even brilliant drumming (or bacon) will only get you so far. You can appreciate a drum solo for about 30 seconds. After that it goes rapidly downhill; likewise a meal that's entirely bacon. (I know, I've tried the Atkins diet.)

John Deacon (the bassist) is your beans. Again, essential. Again, it's got to be right; but it's hard to screw it up and even a magnificent contribution is only so good.

KNOW YOUR CHIPS

A Spotter's Guide To The Basic Chip Archetypes

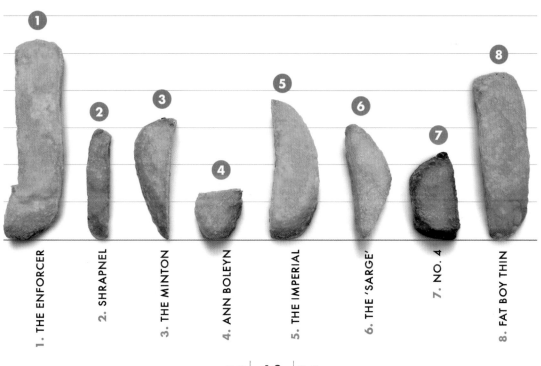

1. THE ENFORCER

2. SHRAPNEL

3. THE MINTON

4. ANN BOLEYN

5. THE IMPERIAL

6. THE 'SARGE'

7. NO. 4

8. FAT BOY THIN

Brian May (the guitarist and Anita Dobson spouse and look-alike) is the egg. It's a bit flashy. It can do a lot of different things, and for a while it can make a real difference, but it can't sustain your attention for long. Man cannot live on eggs alone. (I know, I've tried the Atkins diet.)

Freddie Mercury is the chips. Or was. He made the difference. He made them sound like Queen. Queen with George Michael sounded mostly like George Michael. Queen with that new old bloke from Free just sound like a band with some bloke from Free. The chips make the difference.

That's the first Essential Law Of Chip Contribution To The EBCB Experience. Chips add variety. Chips make the difference. Chips help you tell one EBC&B from another. And with familiarity and practice you'll soon be able to work out where you are if you're ever kidnapped, held in a darkened room and fed fry-ups from a local cafe. So it's worth taking the time to copy this chapter onto rice paper and secrete it in your underwear.

WHY CHIPS ARE NICE

'The French fry, properly executed, provides an ideal interaction between substance (starch), medium (fat or oil), and technique (high heat immersion), resulting in a product that is uniform in all its sensory attributes – the characteristic flavour, aroma, colour, and texture of fried foods that are so widely appealing.'…

'No intermediary coating or wrapping is required; immersed in boiling oil or fat, properly sliced potatoes achieve the exemplary form of a deep-fried food. The outer surfaces are instantly sealed and slowly browned, with all the flavour, colour and crispness that fried starch provides, while the inside portion is cooked to a melting softness. The result offers the textural pleasure of crispness and softness in each golden bite.'

The Primal Cheeseburger – Elisabeth Rozin

STANDARD DEVIATION – THE OTHER FRY-UP POSSIBILITIES

Sausages

Sausages are the cafe blind spot. If you're paying £2.50 for a full English you have to be wary of the sausage. It's likely to be mostly asbestos and tar. Cheap bacon is still very bacon-y and it can still be nice. A cheap sausage is often a thin tube of disaster wrapped in a malicious skin. It can very easily go wrong.

Tomatoes

I just don't get the fried tomato. There seems to be no pleasure in it. It's just a flavourless balloon of superheated water under immense pressure. I assume fried tomatoes are simply a way for British Nuclear Fuels to get rid of the water they use to cool fuel rods. They get little red rubbery pods, pump them up with high temperature water then ship them in special sealed flasks to the cafes of the kingdom. You know those convoys of army trucks you occasionally see trundling down the motorway at a steady 50mph, they're delivering fried tomatoes to cafes.

Mushrooms

Mushrooms are, let's face it, a vegetable. However fried they might be. However 'meaty' they might taste, they're still a vegetable and hence have no place in a man's meal. (I don't mean to be sexist when I say that, when I say man I mean 'right-thinking person'. Hmmm. That's no better, is it.)

Toast

Firstly, I will concede that toast is delicious. The perfect accompaniment to a good fry-up.

But then I will point out that someone has already written a marvellous book about toast. He's called Nick Parker and it's called *Toast*. In there you can learn splendid things like the fact that during the 1930s the Electrical Development Agency promoted toast and 'the electric breakfast' as a way of boosting the use of the national grid during quiet times. Or that toast got put back on the national culinary map during the Second World War – as a way to use up old bread.

Fried Slice

Fried bread is like the devil's toast. It must be very bad for you, all that fat being soaked into the bready sponge. No wonder it's so delicious. But it's where I draw my personal healthiness line. I figure that if I have fried bread as well as everything else I may as well put ice-cream on my bacon and inject sugar directly into my veins. But every now and then, my word, ooh that fried bread.

Black Pudding

The black pudding is a stupendous thing; a dense mass of bloody goodness, secret and black with granular hints of things you don't want to know about. That's probably what gives it its dark power, its demonic allure; we don't know exactly what it's made of, but we suspect that some of it's evil. I'm often tempted by the black pudding and I sometimes succumb, but it's not something you can find everywhere so it's not muscled its way into the book.

Top Five Cafe Sounds

1. The distant sound of drilling. There's nothing like the sense that hard manual labour is happening somewhere else to make you appreciate sitting on your arse, enjoying a fry-up.
2. Frying-up. Obviously.
3. That terrifying scream of steam you sometimes get from the espresso machine – as if The Flying Scotsman was trying to excrete all its awesome twentieth century power into a tiny Italian cup.
4. A badly tuned radio. Ideally something nostalgic and poppy. (Though the New Piccadilly always used to put The Archers on which was a splendid idea.)
5. The innocent laughter of tiny children. Outside. Not bothering you in here.

Top Five Cafe Smells

1. Bacon. Obviously.
2. Coffee. Equally obviously.
3. Ammonia. Less obvious, but it suggests that someone's done some cleaning at some point. Which is good.
4. A moist Daily Express.
5. Cigarette smoke – endlessly recirculated by a creaky old fan.

SITTING, THINKING, CHATTING, LAUGHING

3

A beautiful sign. Simple and informative. We're a cafe and we have plates and cutlery. This sign is a good sign.

THE 192 CAFE / 192 OLD KENT ROAD, SE1

The 192 cafe is a brilliant example of the everyday cafe done dead well. Busy, friendly, cheap and interesting. All sorts of people eating large piles of nice food.

1. They do a nice line in signage at the 192 and handy pictures of egg on toast, in case you don't remember what it looks like. This kind of exuberant signage is welcome in a cafe – they're trying to sell you stuff, which shows they care.

2. This is a bit dark isn't it? Sorry about that. I was defeated by the technical challenge of shooting into the light. But what you might be able to make out is a very comprehensive condiment selection. Nice work 192.

3. And a nice bold slogan – 'so good the competition can't compete' which means they're not the competition, so maybe they can compete after all, but then they become the competition again, so they can't compete. Arrggh. And on and on I go with annoying literalism.

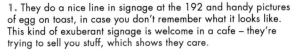

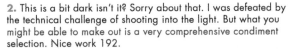

4. A top example of an EBC&B, gorgeously sloppy egg, nice crisp chips, succulent bacon and a generous portion of beans tipping right over the edge. It doesn't get much better than this.

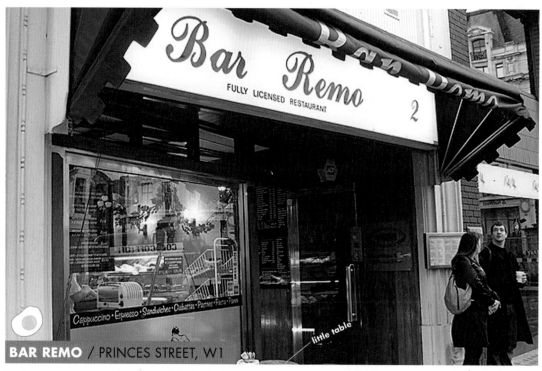

little table

BAR REMO / PRINCES STREET, W1

Bar Remo is a gorgeous place, around the back of Oxford Circus. Very handy when you're doing your big Christmas shopping. It's huge inside, bigger than it looks. More of a restaurant than a cafe really, Mostly very Italian – pasta and sandwiches and stuff. And large hams hanging from the ceiling. And you get those nice baskety place-mats which gives it a note of quality. And you get huge piles of lovely food. Don't go in here if your diet lifestyle revolves around portion control. Also; note the little table outside, it's a perfect place to pose with an espresso and watch the world go by.

1. They do a magnificent egg, bacon, chips and beans. Corpulent chips, pink, curly bacon, and an avalanche of beans sliding over the eggy island. Or something. Anyway, it's very nice. The chip wall looks a little like one of the dams in *The Dambusters* – the egg and beans forming the lake and the bacon the hillside they have to climb steeply over.

2. A luxury condiment line-up. Heinz ketchup. HP sauce. A stuffed bowl of sugar and sweeteners. Salt and pepper. And your own napkin dispenser. You can take as many as you want, no questions asked. You can tell you're in the middle of the profligate south. Condiment supplies don't get much more generous than this.

3. And, because it's very close to lots of theatres, there are tons of slightly faded pictures of slightly faded celebs. You can spend a very pleasant few minutes trying to work out who they are without looking at their signatures. And then you can spend a few more minutes working out who they are after you've seen their signature. I've always wondered how this works. Do faded celebs always carry glossy photos around with themselves? If I did that, would they put my picture up?

4. One of those splendidly ornate decors. Suggestions of ski-ing and romance and Medieval hunting lodges. Lots of brown wood and warm gold lighting.

What is a more perfect environment for a bunch of teenagers to waste time? The invention of the semi-circular booth was the greatest contribution to teenage social intercourse since the development of sarcasm.

NATIONAL MILK BAR / PENRALLT STREET, MACHYNLLETH, POWYS

The National Milk Bar in Mac is one of a small chain set up in Wales by milk producers as an outlet for their products. The fact that they're still going is a testament to Welsh good sense.

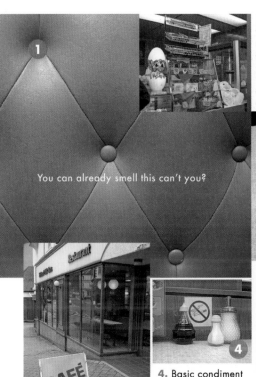

You can already smell this can't you?

CAFÉ OPEN

2. The EBC&B is very special – enhanced by the fantastic patterns on the crockery and the table. And by the delicate placement of sauce sachets. The way the chips pile on top of the egg show what a geneous meal this is, there's not enough room on the plate. And I like the way that one chip has dived straight into the beans, covering itself enthusiastically in beanjuice. A good amount of bacon too, and that great combination of non-crispiness with occasional carbonisation which gives you all the flavours.

3. It's the latest thing – the bench seats tip-up for easy cleaning.

4. Basic condiment set-up, all pleasingly round at the bottom, like many Welsh people.

5. It's always good to recognise the idiosyncrasies of cafe policy. In here, you only get waitress service if you sit on the left. On the right, it's self-service. I don't know what they'd do if you ordered a cooked meal and then moved to the right. Kill you probably.

GINO'S COFFEE BAR / MARYLEBONE PLACE, NW1

Gino's is a brilliant place opposite Marylebone Station. The EBC&B is magnificent, and it's delivered at a hundred miles an hour. Really speedy with no lack of quality. They're obviously used to people trying to catch a train so there are all sorts of posters around the place offering specific speed pledges. So, almost before you've ordered you get big, fat chips, a lovely sloppy egg, bacon hiding ready to surprise you and a good lashing of beans.

1. But the best thing about this place, apart from the friendly efficiency, is the exuberant use of colour and signs. It's a really welcome alternative to drab modernism or tasteful corporate conservatism. It's what you get when an entrepreneurial spirit meets a computer, a colour printer and a laminating machine.

2. Look at those dispensers. Blue pepper. Yellow salt. Who'd have thunk it?

3. Great stools for gazing out at the commuters. They somehow give out this intellectual vibe. It's a place where you could read a novel in French or German and encourage your *fin de siècle ennui* and *Weltschmertz*.

And then of course, when you're finished with the fry-up. You see this and you decide you'll take the rest of the day off and work your way slowly through it.

DELICATE ESSENCE & THE RAMBLERS REST TEAROOMS / HIGH ST., BURNTISLAND

The Delicate Essence is a superb tearoom with an even better name. It's big, light, clean and airy but it still makes you feel like you've stepped into the past. A past where big cakes and big fry-ups were compulsory – not a sin.

1. The EBC&B is a triumph; two textbook eggs, continent-sized slabs of delicious bacon, not many chips but every one is perfect and a beany knoll perched atop the plate.

2. The place is so pleasant and genteel. The old radio and the lovely crockery make ordering an EBC&B feel almost vulgar. You feel you should really order a huge plate of finger cakes and a vast pot of tea.
I love the vibe of this place. Senior citizens having a laugh, rebellious youth having a smoke; it welcomes them all in its capacious bosom.

dribbles

SANDWICH BAR / BROOKS MEWS, W1

The Sandwich Bar is a temple to plain utilitarianism, simple decor and functional food. Big, gorgeous chips like bars of Pharaoh's gold and succulent beans, almost over the edge of the plate. And an egg with the merest hint of yellow. The bacon; fat and juicy and good. And look, I managed to get those tea dribbles down my mug which speak of the bounty of overfilling.

1. A tiny front door belies the size inside. It's not quite the TARDIS. More a big room with a small door. Marvellous sign though. Beautiful plumage.

2. No-one in here really looks happy, but they are. They're happy in a face full of food, *Daily Mirror* crossword, not got to go back to work for forty minutes, kind of way.

3. You look past the tables and into the store-room. Looks rather sparse, it says efficiency to me.

4. An area of outstanding utility. Stuff gets done here.

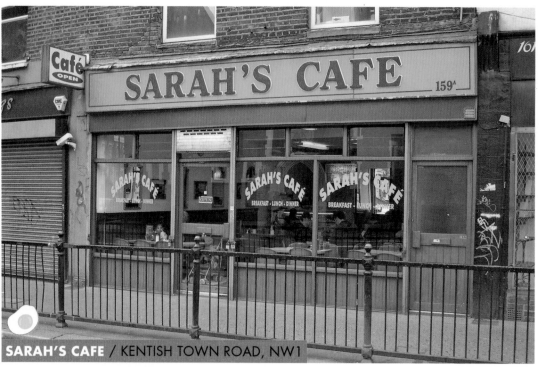

SARAH'S CAFE / KENTISH TOWN ROAD, NW1

There's a gorgeous song called *Mario's Cafe* by the band Saint Etienne. Thousands of years ago we lived not far from Mario's and used to be there fairly regularly. So one day we went back for a visit and discovered that Mario's has got done up (rather like the area). This is, of course, to be hugely applauded – cafe owners have to do what they can to survive – but it meant they were no longer doing the EBC&B. So we went to visit Sarah's instead, which turned out to be brilliant too.

look, here it is!

1. And Sarah's is one of the very few cafes that has egg, bacon, chips and beans, as a set meal on the menu. In that order. Can you see it up there? Thank you Sarah's.

2. It's a top EBC&B; sprawling across a huge oval plate. Lots and lots of crunchy little chips, like a school of whitebait, a nice pool of beans and quality baconage and eggage. I especially like the big red checks on the table, gives everything a slight sense that you're eating inside the digital world of the sci-fi film *Tron*.

3. Actually this is even more Tronlike; condiments as digital skyscrapers on a virtual landscape.

4. This is a great place. Quite big, a basic, no-frills cafe, but done really well. With a real sense that they care and they've made an effort. Clean and nice. Look at this warm, appealing menu. Including lovely puds.

5. And classy decor – none of your tacky posters here – just quality art and mirrors.

BURGER

BURGER
BURGER & CHIPS
1/4 POUNDER
1/4 POUNDER & CHEESE
1/4 POUNDER WITH CHEESE & CHIPS
ROAST CHICKEN CHIPS
1/2 POUNDER
1/2 POUNDER & CHIPS
CHICKEN BURGER
CHICKEN BURGER & CHIPS
BEAN BURGER
BEAN BURGER & CHIPS
VEG BURGER CHIPS
CHIPS

BREAKFAST

SET 1
EGG BACON SAUSAGE
BEANS 2 SLICES

SET 2
EGG BACON SAUSAGE BEANS
BLACK PUDDING 2 SLICES

SET 3
EGG BACON SAUSAGE BEANS
CHIPS MUSHROOMS 2 SLICES

FISH

2.20	PLAICE CHIPS PEAS
3.00	COD CHIPS PEAS
2.50	SCAMPI CHIPS PEAS
2.80	COD BURGER
3.80	COD BURGER CHIPS

OMLET

3.60	PLAIN OMLET CHIPS
4.60	CHEESE OMLET CHIPS
2.60	MUSH.OMLET CHIPS
3.60	HAM.OMLET CHIPS

ON TOST

2.60	
3.60	SCRAMBLED ON 2 TOST
3.60	2 EGG'S ON 2 TOST
1.00	BEANS ON 2 TOST
	CHEESE ON 2 TOST
	MUSHROOM ON 2 TOST

PIES

4.50	STEAK KIDNEY
4.50	CHICKEN MUSHROOM
4.00	BEEF ONION
2.60	SERVED-CHIPS-BEANS
3.60	

SANDWICHES

	Roll	
HAM	1.70	1.30
3.80 CHEESE	1.70	1.30
4.00 CORNED BEEF	1.70	1.30
4.00 TUNA	1.70	1.30
SAUSAGE	1.70	1.30
2.50 EGG	1.70	1.30

SALADS

2.50	
2.50	TUNA SALAD	3.50
2.50	HAM SALAD	3.50
2.50	CHEESE SALAD	3.50

JACKET POTATOES

PLAIN	2.50	2.50
CHEES	3.00	3.00
BEANS	3.80	3.00
HAM		3.00
TUNA		3.00
MUSHROOMS		3.00
EXTRA TOPING	0.70	0.70

DRINKS

TEA	0.70
COFFEE	0.80
CAPPUCCINO	1.30
LEMON TEA	0.80
CAN DRINKS	0.70

SKY
Cafe & Restaurant

SKY 2 / HANSON STREET, W1

Sky 2 is just around the corner from where we live. So I'm in here a lot. Almost every work day. I don't have the full EBC&B every day though, my waistline won't support it, I go for the Atkins version (no chips) and it sees me nicely through to lunchtime.

They're the nicest people and you get a good mix in here. There's always loads of rozzers for some reason, which I always think is the sign of a good cafe. Oh, and don't focus on the spelling, focus on the friendliness.

1. Lovely. Generous portions. Nice crunchy chips. Everything has its place, nothing on top of anything else...
And it's finished. But, oops. the playmobil man's had a heart attack.

3. For some reason this makes me think of a Victorian family portrait. Pa is the brown sauce. Mama is the sugar and the various children are assembled around them, (with Great Uncle Ketchup to one side). And they're all obviously enormously proud of their new menu backdrop.

4. They sell Irn-Bru you know.

Inscrutable cafe art

2. Lots of yellow. Interior designers might run from it, but it works for me.

FORTE'S RESTAURANT / 15 HIDE HILL, BERWICK-UPON-TWEED

I love the peculiarities of ordering the EBC&B. Lots of places you can't get it because they don't do chips. Some places you have to negotiate variants on their set breakfast. Here you have to get a bacon and egg bun – and then add some chips and beans. Perfectly fair. And actually a splendid meal. The extra bread is lovely. The chips are fat and crisp, the beans nicely positioned with lots of juice. And tidying up the bacon and egg in the bun makes a degree of aesthetic sense.

1. This place has got everything. It's lovely. Friendly. Charming. Tasty food. Great signage.

2. I love these busy counters. All sorts of stuff available. Everything you could want. Ice-cream. Sweeties. And those great food photos on the back wall. Looks like they were shot at some point in the 70s.

3. I told you this place has everything – a huge magnificent mural of some people at a different cafe, somewhere else. So if you don't like this cafe, you can pretend to be at a different one. Two cafes for the price of one.

4. Another of those great things about cafes – the odd places they keep the loos, and they way they direct you to them.

5. They've got these fantastic fast food trays. From the proud and noble era when fast food wasn't a dirty idea – just a convenient innovation.

REGENCY CAFE / 17-19 REGENCY STREET, SW1

The Regency is brilliant. Huge and spacious and tiled and magnificent. They're famous for their shouting. They holler out the orders at huge volume, which all just adds to the atmosphere.

1. I think this is most beautiful condiment display I've ever seen. So simple and right it almost makes you cry.

2. This EBC&B rocks. High quality. And a visual feast as well as a mouthy one. The egg is pale and interesting while the bacon's dark and mysterious. The chips exude the golden light of summer evening; the beans, the wistfulness of autumn. And you thought it was just a fry-up.

THANKS FOR FRANKS / 26 FOUBERT'S PLACE, W1

Thanks For Franks proves that a great cafe is a viable modern business. They've updated the look, added some psychedelia, some US diner vibe and they do good, simple food. And they're nice.

1. The fry-up is a classic, made even nicer because you can sit outside and eat it. Pretending you're French or something. They're very generous with the chips, the egg is gorgeously golden, the bacon delightful, the beans a hidden surprise.

2. There's a lot of blue inside. Blue's clearly a theme. That and shininess.

3. Their splendid food and friendly faces have made them award winners. And, they're not shy of telling you about it. But that's fair enough. One of the reasons they're good is they put some energy into what they do. And they're proud of it. Highly recommended for a tasty, energetic feed.

10AM ETERNAL

MY FAVOURITE CAFE time is about 10 am.

The breakfast rush is over but the radio's still blaring away and there's a bit of energy to the place. And it feels like everyone there is skiving in one way or another.

There'll be a couple of pensioners reading the paper and chatting. There'll be three blokes in high-viz jackets having their morning tea break. There'll be someone doing the *Daily Mirror* crossword and several people gazing blankly into space. There's always someone who's unmistakably a freelance designer having a furtive coffee – you never have time off when your time's your own. The only hints of stress come from the young woman near the door who's clearly got an interview coming up at the company round the corner; and from the psycho killer in the corner – the mad, muttering man who everyone tries to ignore.

This is when a cafe's at its best. You can tune into most of the conversations around you without needing to flap your ears too much. You can nurse a single cup of tea without feeling too guilty and you can keep reminding yourself that you're not at work either. Hurrah. You have an excuse (funeral / dentists / rabies / meteorite impact / conference) and you can sit and plan the rest of your work-free day.

You notice the little things at 10 am. Like the door of Lino's near Tottenham Court Road. The door opens inwards and it's been hung so it misses the front counter by just a couple of millimetres. That's precision door-hanging. That's making the most of limited space.

Or you notice the spellings on the menu in Sky 2 – Omlet. Tost.

And, particularly, you find time to notice the pictures on the wall; the celebrity endorsements, the signed 8 x 4s.

Bar Remo near Oxford Circus and 'London's Theatreland' is a great place for tracking the hierarchies of celebrity. The walls are festooned with nicely framed and signed celebrity glossies. But there seems to be no celebrity filter, no sense of who's actually famous or more famous or not famous anymore. A random sampling in the Bar Remo includes The Shadows, Graham Norton, Alan Whicker, Ron Moody, Tony Robinson, Tom Courtney, Ray Allan and Lord Charles and Sophia Loren. Plus, of course, The Bloke Who Played Nick Cotton on *EastEnders*, Someone Who Might Be Michelle Dotrice If I Could Remember Exactly Who She Was and, obviously, Her From *Crossroads*.

I've always wondered about the etiquette of this kind of stuff. Do celebs always carry pictures around with them? Do they offer them to cafe owners when they're on the way up – as a sign that they've arrived or do cafe owners pester them for pictures? Do you get some sort of discount if you proffer a picture? Could I get my picture put up if I just carried one around with 'All the best, Russell' already written on it?

Then you sit and notice all the peculiar signage that people stick up. The rules and assertions and set breakfasts that people decide are important.

This is one of the most compelling and essential things about cafes. They're independent, normally managed by the owners and they can make their own rules. And they can get very particular about the way things are done.

The Grindleford Station cafe is notorious for this. There are hand-scribbled signs everywhere telling you what is and isn't allowed. No coach parties. No dogs. Take your pots over here when they're done. No, not over there, over here. Don't do this. Make sure you do that. Don't ask for change. Blah, blah, blah. People can easily take offence at this but I like the individualism it connotes. Much better than the bland corporate requests not to smoke ('because it impairs the flavour of our coffee') or the regular use of the word 'patrons'. When do you ever hear people referred to as patrons except on signs in cafes?

Vecchio's Snack Bar in Llandudno has a similar approach – but you get the sense it's a bit more reactive – each note is a response to a particular incident – 'No Dogs' 'No Prams or Pushchairs' 'We Regret That Persons Bringing Their Own Food Cannot Be Served.' I'm particularly fond of the last one. You can imagine the drama that preceded it. Some holidaying family caught in the Welsh rain decide to have their picnic in Vecchio's and supplement it with a Horlicks or two. Mr Vecchio takes understandable umbrage at this transgression and dashes off another note in very firm marker pen. I bet it made him feel a lot better.

And then of course, comes the computer. Being savvy business people cafe owners have embraced the

personal computer and are constantly churning out new signage with their printer and occasionally a laminating machine. Thus you find the Hatton Salt Box proudly boasting that they serve 'real chips' (you know what they mean, but you can't hold wondering if other places serve imaginary chips, like the emperor's new chips) and you get the plethora of set breakfasts at Sky 2 on Hanson Street. Every set menu is accompanied by cute little bits of clip art – sometimes relevant, sometimes not. And a bold, upper case sign states firmly that **'SET MENU CAN NOT BE CHANGED'**; although in my experience they're completely accommodating to whatever you want to order.

But no-one has embraced home signage like Gino's, near Marylebone Station. The places is festooned with all kinds of signs, saying all kinds of things, in all kinds of colours, fonts and sizes. Coloured type, coloured paper, even coloured condiments. Gino's entrepreneurial spirit finds its expression all around the cafe.

I've always wanted to take these cafe habits and import them into my own home. I want to print out a sign saying Bedtime Is 8pm And This Will Not Be Changed, get it laminated and stick it on my son's bedroom door. Or I'd like to have a little sign saying No More Than Three Action Man Toys In The Fish Tank At Any One Time. My wife would probably like to find some clipart of discarded clothes and make a sign saying The Laundry Basket And The Landing Floor Are Not Synonymous. That'd be aimed at me. Or my son, Arthur, could make a sign saying No Sleeping After 5am. Or. Or...

Sorry. I've gone off on a bit of a tangent haven't I? But that's what it's like in a cafe at about 10am. You've time to think. To daydream. To go off on tangents.

WHICH IS THE SOUP SPOON?

THE CAFE CAN be an intimidating environment for the novice. Where should one sit? How much do you tip the maître D? Which one is the soup spoon? Here's a handy guide to cafe etiquette for all you newcomers.

Appropriate Volume – If you're slightly posh you must be as quiet as you can. If you're old and deaf you should be quiet most of the time, but occasionally very loud. If you're a gang of four blokes in high-viz jackets you can be as loud as you want. Children should mostly be quiet except when the rest of the cafe goes suddenly quiet when they should say something like 'Mummy, why does that man have black teeth?' in a loud stage whisper.

Banter – One of the best bits about a cafe is the overheard banter. And this is how you should leave it; overheard. Do not be tempted to join in. You may have a ready riposte which makes Noël Coward look like Noel Edmonds. Keep it to yourself. The only people allowed to banter are the people who've been going there 30 years longer than you.

Condiments – Cafe tables are small. You can reach the condiments for yourself. Don't bother asking to get them passed. Equally, don't bother the waitress for the brown sauce if there's some on a nearby table. She's only serving you to a certain extent, SHE'S NOT YOUR SLAVE.

Constabulary – The forces of law and order love a good cafe and they tend to go mob-handed. Be polite. They may be eating the same food as you but they'll still bang you up if you step out of line.

Computers – You can play games on your phone. You can bang out a carpet-laying estimate on your calculator. But don't get your laptop out. If you want wifi, go to Starbucks.

Cutlery – It may come to you wrapped tightly in a napkin. It may be on some trays up front. It may just get plonked in a pile on the table. All this is acceptable.

Elbows – Put them where you like. On the table. Behind your head. Doesn't matter. If you can though, get something tattooed on one of them. Preferably with a biro.

Enthusiasm – You may well love cafes. You may think the fittings and the signage and the menus are all exquisite. Don't say so. Because you'll be seen as an arse.

Feet – you probably shouldn't put your feet on the table. But you may be able to put them on the chair opposite. However, if you do this, you're expected to shift them if a waitress or anyone comes near, making like they were never there in the first place.

Forks – If your fork doesn't have tiny flecks of dried egg between the tines you're entitled to ask for a replacement.

Frodo Baggins – Don't talk about Lord Of The Rings.

Injuries – Many of the best cafes in the country are next to Casualty departments of large, inner city hospitals. Probably the demand for hot, sweet tea and the need to wait around for bad news. For that reason you'll often notice your fellow patrons are suffering from horrendous and recent injuries. Unless they actually start bleeding in your chips it's best not to say anything.

Mobile phones – Talk on them, let them ring, take photos with them, do what you like. They're part of the reality of modern life and all that tutting about mobile manners that the chattering classes like to do has got to stop. A particular technique that works well in cafes is the dual-audience conversation. You see this happening all the time. While someone is talking to a caller at the end of the line it's tremendously clear that he has another audience in mind. The audience in the cafe. Could be his table mates, could be the whole cafe, but if you can hear then you're entitled to earwig. Enjoy the performance.

Newspapers – You should bring your own paper. Any newspaper is acceptable but if it's a broadsheet everyone will assume you're an arse. If you see a paper you fancy reading then you should point and mutter about it at whoever's nearest. Something like readyourpapermate?

Slurping – the Chinese and Japanese slurp their soup to get more air in it and improve the flavour. Apparently. If it's good enough for them and their soup it's good enough for you and your tea. Though slurping gravy from your plate is probably going too far.

Smoking – tricky one this. The obvious advice is simply to deplore smoking as a dreadful, selfish and anti-lungist activity. It's not big. It's not clever. (Though it often looks quite cool.) But I just can't bring myself to completely believe in no smoking at all in cafes. A little hint of smoke just does something to the atmosphere, something special, especially when so many other places are going smoke-free. The smoke tells you you're somewhere different, somewhere where temporary pleasure is more important than long-term well-being and where working-class culture hasn't yet been marginalised.

Sugar cubes – It is acceptable to let your child build small walls and things with the sugar cubes. But you should make your tip a bit bigger to compensate.

Table choice – In a completely empty cafe you can sit anywhere. Though you'll be expected to divine what the best seat in the house is and sit there. The best seat is probably by a window or a fruit machine or the heater. It's probably away from the draught by the door and not on a major waiter route. It may well have newspapers on it. The patina of varnish will be thinner on this most occupied of chairs but you probably won't be able to tell this until you're sitting down.

In a cafe with people in it you're expected to sit as far away from everyone else as possible – without making it obvious that that's what you're doing. This is quite a subtle art.

If there's only one of you and it's a busy cafe you're expected to try and find a table for one, or at best two. If you occupy a four-person table when there's a two-er available expect the strongest sanction the redoubtable British bulldog can deliver – strong stares and a barely audible tut. If you can withstand that kind of opprobrium then you can probably get away with anything.

In a very busy cafe you may be forced into that most perilous and uncomfortable of situations – sharing a table with a stranger. Rule One – Don't Panic. You can do this if you remember a few simple rules. Firstly, keep eye contact and conversation to an absolute minimum. If you do need to communicate then do so without using actual words. For instance, you'll probably need to grunt something like 'isthiseatakenmate?' when you sit down. Secondly, as soon as a second person sits down then that table has a rigid dividing line right down the middle. You may have sprawled out with your paper before, well not now, now you have to withdraw to your side of the demarcation line, preferably leaving a demilitarized zone in the middle.

If there are no tables at all available then leave. There's no point just hanging about. Go and find another cafe. There are loads of them.

Tea Bags – Quite often you'll get your tea brought to you with the teabag still in it. There may or may not be somewhere to put the bag before you sip. If there's a saucer, use that. If there isn't then there's no acceptable choice but to put it on the table.

Television – Occasionally you'll find a cafe with a telly glaring away silently in the corner; if you're lucky with the subtitling on. Just stare at it mindlessly the whole time you're there. You have no choice. It's television.

Final note – If you're a big bloke who's just finished half a day of genuinely hard labour, or a traffic warden who's spent her whole day on her feet, or a pensioner who's just trying to keep warm, none of this is applicable to you. You can do what you like.

But enough of this frivolity, look at the size of that spout

THE SACHET GALLERY

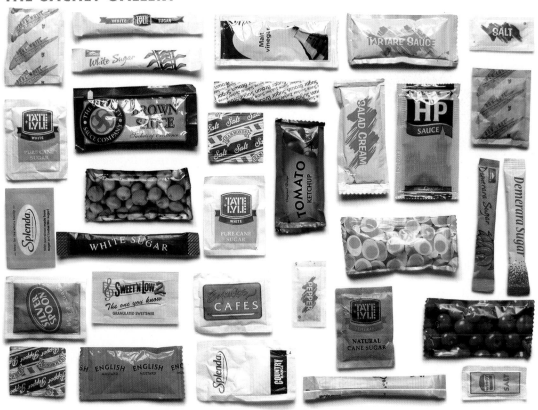

THE THIN LINE BETWEEN SAUCE AND NOT-SAUCE

ALTHOUGH THIS BOOK is called *Egg Bacon Chips & Beans*; the real hero is probably sauce. Specifically (in my case) brown sauce.

1. Sauce is good because it's a smelly liquid

It gets flavour to us quickly and powerfully. To quote Len Fisher in *How To Dunk A Doughtnut*, 'We often enhance the aromatic appeal of our meals prior to indigestion by coating them with gravy and sauces. Because of their liquid constituency, these materials release their aromas more readily than do the foods they coat, and provide an enhanced aroma experience and flavour expectation even before the food reaches the mouth.'

So, sauce makes the meal exciting. It creates the expectation, it gets the nose working. All because it's a slimy liquid.

Now I'll bow to no-one in my admiration of the EBC&B but it definitely needs something to give it a little kick. And that's where the brown sauce comes in. The sauce supplies the astringent, tasty hit of sour.

2. Ketchup just is

Malcolm Gladwell (he of *The Tipping Point* and *Blink*) has written a long and fascinating article about Ketchup which points out just what a strange substance it is.

His key point is that Ketchup doesn't work like other foods. Its peculiar combination of ingredients and flavours has to work in just the right way (balancing vinegar, salt, tomato, sweet and sour) otherwise it doesn't work at all. And that means that you can't really create good ketchup varieties. Which is why you don't get all the different types like you do with Pasta Sauce or Mustard.

3. There's a thin line between sauce and not sauce

The above point about Ketchup is illustrated when you go to a cafe and get a cheaper brand of sauce served up to you. You notice that they're a little more liquid, a bit more vinegary. They have more bite but they don't enhance the meal so much. They've crossed the line and become flavoured vinegar. Or something.

4. Sauce is all about control (as Janet Jackson once almost sang)

We like sauce because we can self-medicate. We determine how much we have and where it goes. And, of course, we use this control to express our personalities. We may be a 'splurge it all over the place' person, or a 'make a pile in the corner' person. We may get one big glomp designed to last the whole meal or we may keep going back for another dose. It's entirely up to us. It's our inalienable right to do this, whatever the bureaucrats in Brussels tell us.

5. HP Sauce and Daddies sauce are owned by Heinz

And that's weird and scary. Shouldn't the EU be worried about this? Yes, Microsoft may have a bit of a monopoly with computers but how could Heinz own both HP and Daddies? That can't be right. Not just because of the potential for holding the nation to ransom by controlling the sauce supply but because it goes against our 'folk understanding' of how brands work.

Because in my little head (and I suspect lots of other people's) it works like this:

HP Sauce is made by men in bowler hats in the cellars of the Houses Of Parliament. The ingredients are obviously all brown, but they're quite posh; things like Church's shoes, hunting dogs, oak trees, cigars, and old copies of the Book of Common Prayer, that kind of thing. Then I imagine an extremely old retainer in a big white wig tests each bottle by reciting Latin incantations over it and glaring at it through a monocle. The bottles are then delivered to stores around the country by the steam train out of Camberwick Green.

Daddies Sauce, on the other hand, is manufactured in a huge, smoky factory in the West Midlands by gnomes and dwarves who spend their evenings watching *The Loneliness Of The Long Distance Runner* and *Saturday Night, Sunday Morning*. Daddies is made from conkers, old boots, bricks, mud and Newcastle Brown Ale. It's flavoured by being used to wash front-steps in the Black Country before being re-collected and squirted into bottles by pit ponies and children.

They are both, of course, equally delicious. But can you see what I'm getting at? HP is posh. Daddies is common. They shouldn't come from the same place.

Because that's the class structure of sauce. Daddies is working class. Ketchup is middle class. HP is upper-class. (Just like classic class politics – the peasantry and the aristocracy unified against the merchants)

And yet, in reality, they're all controlled from some well-appointed Heinz marketing suite somewhere, probably Slough.

What a world we live in.

6. There's something fantastic and alien about those big catering bottles of sauce you sometimes see – they speak of another world

You know the ones. Huge, often dripping with vinegar, which has made the label go all transparent. I like them because they're so strangely alien. They speak of a world that you're never going to see; the world of the cafe cash and carry, the world of catering supplies. I once decided that I wanted to visit a cash and carry so as to help me understand the economics and logistics of cafes.

But I didn't. The thing is, I just didn't want to see behind the curtain. I wanted to keep my cash and carry fantasies in place. Because my vision of these places is very fixed and very important to me.

I see a huge out of town shopping development occupied mostly by massive retail sheds, though with an occasional Pizza Hut and bowling arena for light relief. There's an even bigger shed, with even less enticing signage. It has an air of impenetrability. Like Fort Knox or Milton Keynes. To get in you have to show a card you borrowed off your cousin.

There are enormous shelves everywhere, stretching way into the distance. It's like an even more massive version of the government storage facility at the end of Indiana Jones. But these shelves aren't carrying secret government files or wardrobes called Knobb, they're carrying catering supplies. You're in a world of sauce. Enough ketchup to sink the Titanic. Enough brown sauce to sink the iceberg.

Now you can die happy.

4

LOVELY, LOVELY, LOVELY

tiny sausage mountain

CHERRYTOP CAFE / PADDINGTON STREET, W1

I love the Cherrytop Cafe. On the surface it's just another cafe, but if you take the time to look you'll see a really special place, a place that puts real effort and care into what they do. And there's a lovely warm glow to the place. Wood, nice lights, lots of glass and a purple monster thing ruling over the counter.

1. Look at that fry-up to start with: I've never seen a neater EBC&B, everything is lined up with military precision, smart rows of foodstuff presented for your delectation. And they're not just neat, they're deeply tasty too. Then take a second to examine that egg more closely – they've constructed an elaborate latticework of white over the yolk. I've never seen that before either, I can't imagine what alchemical processes made that possible.

2. A lovely simple condiment display, with a generously stuffed sugar sachet bowl and nice full salt and pepper. No need to reach for anyone else's. See the attention to detail?

3. There's a note of quality in the fixings. This isn't your bargain basement placemat or mug. There's a nice floral theme, and nice heavy knifes and forks. Lovely.

4. And the care extends to a smart bit of entrepreneurialism, a big sign in the window pointing out that an enormous fry-up counts as a diet meal in Dr Atkins' world. Good work Cherrytop Cafe.

HARRIS'S CAFEREST / GOLDHAWK ROAD, W12

It's a fantastic place. Great signage and splendidly ancient people. The colours inside are fantastic.
Glowing with imperial optimism.

1. Those lace curtains are special: they give it a 50s homeliness you can't resist. They make you feel like all's right with the world. Like the Old King will go on forever and the British will be first on the moon.

2. The condiments are textbook. Look at the size of that salt cellar. There's probably Dickensian salt in there.

3. No, this is not me eating by a mirror. This is two EBC&Bs on one table. Marvellous. A good egg – very white and very yellow. Deep, rich beans. Loads of chips, some of them very small, almost nano-chips. (Possibly the chips of the future?) Super soggy bacon with a hint of carbonisation. And my companion pronounced the EBC&B excellent.

NEW PICCADILLY / DENMAN STREET, W1

Look at that welcoming glow.

Sample conversations between staff and regulars when I was in there; how evil VAT was (and Westminster council seemed to get a lot of the blame for that which is a little harsh), how the Dutch invented VAT, or maybe it was the French, the activities of Frederick the Great, falling asleep on the bus and waking up in Poole, how the New Piccadilly keeps being featured in glossy magazines (mostly *Mademoiselle*), how someone came in to try and get it listed and how Lorenzo would try and sell it first.

The New Piccadilly has featured in many magazines, books, ads and films and there are loving tributes to it on several websites. But it has its own champion and laureate in Adrian Maddox, author of the book *Classic Cafes*, you can see many more gorgeous pictures of the place at his website www.classiccafes.co.uk.

1. A typically individual take on the EBC&B from the New Piccadilly, nice chips and very curly bacon, it's those almost American crunchy bits of bacon, not the damp slabs that cafes normally love.
Egg nestling away there. Beans almost over the edge of the plate. Marvellous. I tell you what though, those brilliant yellow tables seem to make it hard to shoot the food and make it look delicious. Though a proper photographer probably could.

2. I have very fond memories of the New Piccadilly. and not just because it's an undoubted design classic. Anne and I used to come here in the 80s, when we first moved to London. We'd meet after work at the Criterion at Piccadilly Circus (when you could just sit there and have a coffee and a croissant in that incredible room) and then just wonder around Soho in the evening and stop there for something to eat. It was cheap, welcoming and always full of interesting people. Plus, we really liked the 'EATS' sign in the window.
It reminded us of America.

ROSSI'S / HANBURY STREET, E1

Rossi's is a delightful place near Spitalfields. Big and friendly and welcoming. And a good mixed crowd of all sorts of people.

1. This area has gone from being a place where people worked to a place where some people work, many people shop and young people go out for a drink in the evening. You can tell that from the beer bottle balanced on the window sill.

2. The biggest sauce bottles you have ever seen. And a vaguely young person in a vaguely young person t-shirt. Places like Rossi's are great because everyone ends up there – trendies and tradesmen, skivers and scholars.

3. The EBC&B is great. Big slabs of bacon. Sharp chips. Glowing beans. Sumptuous egg.

4. I like all the wood and the metal tables. It's not 'classic' – but it's warm, friendly and practical.

SELLY SAUSAGE / 539 BRISTOL ROAD, SELLY OAK, BIRMINGHAM

The Selly Sausage is not a traditional cafe, but it is a great one. It's slap in the centre of Birmingham's student quarter and it knows its market very well – cheap, decent food, parties and music and a graphic style that seems to incorporate everything students have ever been interested in.

2. A textbook condiment collection. And they're very smart with the cutlery, leaving a canteen of knives, forks etc on the table so you can just grab what you need. You get the impression that this place has very well thought out systems – it probably needs them since a large proportion of both staff and customers will be slightly unfocused students.

1. You can see the eclectic decorative scheme – there's Mao up there, and the Statue Of Liberty, and some random graffiti.

4. Another genius systems innovation, they sound the horn when an order's ready. It's efficient and it completely delights any four-year olds you might have with you.

3. I suspect this is a combination they don't get asked for a lot, but they didn't blink and they rose to the challenge with considerable aplomb. Curly fries are a great way of ringing the chippy changes and look at the plump rounded quality of that egg. A simple, handsome rasher of bacon and a little sea of beans. If this is what our students are eating then the nation's future is in safe hands and we'll all get our pensions paid for.

Like an Edward Hopper painting, but cheerful and mouthwatering

THE SHEPHERDESS / 221 CITY ROAD EC1

The Shepherdess is a bit of an institution. It's many people's favourite cafe. And you can see why just looking at that welcoming glow; the warming lights serve to get your stomach fired up as you approach for a pre-work fry-up.

1. The grub is top-notch. The chips are golden and crunchy, the bacon tasty, the egg delicious and every bean is a little parcel of orange loveliness. And it's all crammed companionably on the plate.

2. Condiment 101. All your bases covered. And the menu. And napkins. You are good to go.

3. Then in the middle there's this slightly strange garden furniture, which adds a touch more character. And the kitchen hatch has a bizarre Tyrolean style roof. I guess it might be to do with the Shepherdess theme. Like the green walls (are they supposed to be like grass?)

Continued...

4. And a counter equipped with everything you could possibly need for a happy and stress-free life.

5. The lovely colour of these tables makes everything look scrumptious. Which is why we chose an EBC&B from the Shepherdess as the cover for this book.

7. Painted-on curtains are more practical and more stylish.

6. The waitresses really do move this fast.

8. A high density of high-viz jackets is always a sign of a good cafe.

SUNSHINE CAFE / 125 LARK LANE, LIVERPOOL

Lark Lane is a really interesting street near Sefton Park in Liverpool. It's a great mix of traditional neighbourhood, bohemian quarter and funky district. Interesting shops. Lots of cafes, restaurants and characters. It's bright, warm and friendly.

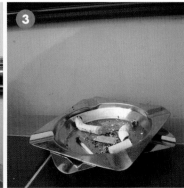

1. They do a very substantial EBC&B. Tons of crunchy chips, big slabs of bacon, nicely reduced beans, a pleasantly shy egg.

2. Basic condiments. No nonsense. No flim flam. No sell out.

3. This is a great cafe for a smoke. It's a community place so you get a lot of pensioners spending a few pleasant hours with a cup of tea, a chat and a fag.

4. 'Mega breakfast' – the two most beautiful words in the English language.

MEGA BREAKFAST £4

5. I love the embrace of all the generations So many places these days just focus relentlessly on a single demographic group – teens or mums or whatever. But a good cafe is for everyone. The young, the old, the rich, the poor, the workers, the students, the golf professionals.

YORK CAFE / YORK PLACE, CLIFTON, BRISTOL

A special case – the York Cafe is one of only two places in the book I've not visited myself, but so many visitors to the website recommended it I felt we had to cover it. And when a mate of mine (Chris) was heading through Bristol for a Carling Cup final I asked him to pop in. This is his report:

Situated in Clifton about a mile out of Bristol City Centre, York Café is a friendly spot for some EBC&B. It's close to Bristol University and seems to get a mix of students and locals. The booths seat 6 so unless you're a small battalion of eaters be prepared to snuggle up with people you may not know.

1. A generous portion of chips. Crisp and golden on the outside, fluffy on the inside. Nice. The highlight of the EBC&B however was undoubtedly the egg.
Cooked to perfection, the yolk was plump and sweet.
The bacon tasty, the beans good, but as you can see by the beans to juice ratio they perhaps weren't Heinz.

2. Other highlights include the red formica tables, the lime green laminated menus, the spotted dick on the menu and a large fridge containing various items of chocolate confectionery and cans of coke just in case you get peckish on your way to wherever you're headed.

MARIE'S CAFE / LOWER MARSH, WATERLOO

Marie's is a perfect example of what a cafe should be. Lovely friendly people and great food. It's also a splendid example of how cafe culture changes, evolves and improves as new people start to move in and run cafes. You can have a big old British fry-up or a top Thai meal. And they're both very good.

1. The EBC&B has a certain Thai quality – particularly in the egg. Which makes it all the more splendid. Lovely chips too.

2. And there's a Thai feel to the condiments too.

3. The décor is also a blend of traditional British and traditional Thai.

4. The mixed cuisine makes for a splendidly mixed crowd. And it's very near Waterloo so there's a slightly continental feel to it too.

Traffic warden. Always a sign of a good cafe.

MARYLEBONE CAFE / MARYLEBONE LANE, W1

The Marylebone Cafe is an unassuming place not for from the bustly, expensive bits of Mayfair. This place apparently has some history, a correspondent on my website says his parents were proprietors during the 60s and he remembers his Auntie Brenda on the evening news in 1963, crossing Wigmore Street with a tray of tea and biscuits for John Profumo and Christine Keeler who'd just been arrested.

1. A lovely breakfast. And, now you know that Christine Keeler story, doesn't the egg look kind of 60s? Nice texture to the bacon. Great chips, sort of shrapnelly looking. And an inviting sea of beans.

2. I'm hungry. This sign makes me hungry.

3. Enormous pile of ashtrays. None of that no smoking nonsense here.

5. There's nothing quite like cafe art.

4. Looming condiments.

SARAH'S TUCK-IN / GRAINGER MARKET, NEWCASTLE

The Grainger Market is one of those brilliant old indoor markets some towns are lucky to have. It's full of independent traders and craftspeople and folk selling stuff for less than you'd think is possible. And tucked inside, on a corner is the fantastic Sarah's Tuck-In. Nice seating inside and that long row of outside seats, all generously supplied with ashtrays. There's some fine Geordie smoking goes on in here.

1. It's like a Barbra Hepworth sculpture. Pure form. Anything else is unnecessary.

2. A full breakfast at a very reasonable price.

3. Sheer Geordie gorgeousness. A huge quantity of bacon, nice fat chips, the works. This'll fill you up.

Though actually, the milk poster seems to improve it.

4. Look at that, all ready to cook, a lot of food. A big lot of big food.

YOU MUST BE TOUGH AND TIRELESS

THE CLASSIC CAFES of London are marvellous places. They should be preserved like Sites of Special Scientific Interest and guarded by force-fields and wolves.

The seaside cafes, beloved of everyone's youth, must be protected from mega-casinos and lattenisation, if necessary through the imposition of a massive punitive tax on soy milk and chocolate sprinkles.

I believe all this.

I love these places.

Yet the places I love most live by the road. And they don't need our help; they're doing very well without interventions from concerned citizens and miserablist journalists.

Transport cafes are the guardians of the British cafe tradition because they keep that tradition economically viable. They know their customers and they deliver what they want:

1. Cheap food that fills you up quickly.

2. The opportunity to talk to someone; a waitress, a fellow traveller, someone.

3. The opportunity to be left alone; you need a paper, a telly, anything so you can tune people out.

4. A decent loo.

5. A big car park.

A good truck stop delivers all this plus all sorts of more specialist requirements like DERV and pornography. But an excellent truck stop will also deliver particular ambient extras that add a certain piquancy to the experience.

1. None of the chairs will match. The original chairs were bought as a job lot some time in the 70s. They were probably destined for a municipal conference facility but got hijacked somehow. They've now been supplemented with chairs from car boot sales, from skips and from dead people. All perfectly serviceable but unlikely to draw oohs and ahhs from the *Antiques Roadshow* crowd.

2. Everything will be geared to keeping costs down. So there won't be big bottles of HP on the tables. Sauce will be strictly rationed via sachets or heavily diluted with industrial vinegar.

3. Despite the rigorous cost control the portions will be generous. There won't be the skimpiness of your average motorway services. This food has to get you through a long day delivering bulky, heavy stuff; two little rashers won't cut it.

What it means is that when you get to the cafe you're knackered. You get out of the car with a stiff-legged hobble and stumble to the loo to empty your over-full bladder. The tune you were shouting at the top of your voice (to stop yourself falling asleep) is churning round and round in your head, preventing you from thinking any kind of coherent thought. Only some kind of cellular memory, buried deep in your genes, gets you to the counter and gets the words 'full English' out of your mouth.

Hello Mr. Chips

YOU ALSO SERVE;
THE 5 SERVICE PARADIGMS AND HOW TO COPE

BRITISH CULTURE IS not primarily a service culture. It's a waiting culture (not waiting as in waiters and waitresses but as in queuing, standing around, lolling) and a culture of silent complaint.

So we're not good at service. Not good at giving it. Not good at getting it. If the tea takes too long to arrive we'll tut, crane our necks round to look pointedly into the kitchen and maybe even glare at the waitress (while desperately trying not to catch her eye) but it'll be ages before we complain. **THIS IS A GOOD THING**. This is what helps society tick along in a smooth and unembarrassing manner.

However, despite this implicit agreement that service won't be great and we won't complain about it there are times when the service style can be troubling. So here's some handy advice about what to do in the cafe of your choice.

Slow

Slow service is rare in cafes. They mostly want you out of there because they want more bums on seats. And it's not like restaurants where the longer they keep you waiting the more wine you'll drink. But it can happen, especially when they're busy and when this happens the best advice is, well, wait. There's not much else you can do is there? If you make a fuss you might get your meal slightly quicker (though probably not) but the whole cafe will just think you're an arse. So why bother? Read the paper. Do a crossword. Make a mental list of things that are better than they used to be.

Surly

Surliness is part of the theatre of EBC&B (or Théâtre d'Oeuf, Jambon, Frites et Haricots as the French might have it.) So maybe your waitress is a little rude. It's not the end of the world. She has probably had a really rough day. Enjoy it. Revel in it. A lot of these people have brought surliness to imaginative new heights; they are Rostropovichs of Rudeness, Einsteins of the Insult. This could be your chance to be insulted at an Olympic level. And so what if it's just common or garden rudeness? Why ruin your meal? As my nephew would say; take a chill pill. And then, take 10p off the tip.

Random

So, what do you do when you don't get what you order? Live with it. Eat it. You might like it. Life is too predictable today anyway. You've got your Sky Plus and your ipod and your digital radio and your phone all giving you exactly what you want, whenever you want. It's time you had something you didn't want, when you didn't want it. Try something new.

Friendly

Brilliant. Just what you're after. Lovely food and a splendid smiley chat with a member of the waiting community. Quick tip though; if you're a bit lonely (and let's face it, lots of people in cafes are a bit lonely) don't assume that a waitress loves you just because she smiles at you. It's an easy mistake to make and we've all been there.

Too friendly

Possibly the worst scenario. Especially if you're British. What do you do if someone insists on telling you everything about themselves and how it's going and what bastards VAT inspectors are and how Burton Albion got on in the Cup? Especially if they combine it with all sorts of assumptions about what you're interested in or what you care about – like, because you're reading the paper they'll suddenly ask you who won the 3.15 at Uttoxeter, when you might actually be reading a very trenchant analysis of fin de siecle mores in Patagonian Ping Pong culture. What to do? Smile thinly. Return to eating. Never go back.

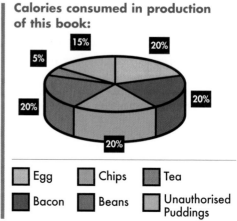

Calories consumed in production of this book:

15%
5%
20%
20%
20%
20%

Egg   Chips   Tea

Bacon   Beans   Unauthorised Puddings

ON THE ROAD

LITTLE CHEF / MARKHAM MOOR, NOTTINGHAMSHIRE

Lots of (unthinking) people will raise their eyebrows at the inclusion of Little Chef in here, but they're wrong. Little Chefs are beloved by many people and they've been a boon for millions of families every year; providing the perfect break in the annual summer holiday hell, driving from Aberdeen to St. Ives in your Ford Anglia.

1. This Little Chef is particularly to be cherished because of its extraordinary design. Originally built as a petrol station, it has a hyperbolic paraboloid roof, designed by an architect called Sam Scorer, it's a graceful assemblage of curves which gives it a lovely, optimistic fifties feeling.

2. The EBC&B is more than decent, with the spin of getting your beans in a decorous bowl – you can imagine an uncertain alien trying to clean his tentacles in there when unsure of the etiquette. Nice, big, fat chips, two highly textured eggs and a generous portion of sloppy pink bacon.

3. They're not going to win any design awards but Little Chefs aren't really about that. And there are too many things trying to win design awards these days. A friendly, practical un-objectionable interior is just what you want.

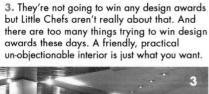

4. I always like the checked curtains in a Little Chef – always shows that however fancy they try to get with their menus, they're still essentially a lower middle-class icon, like all that's best in Britain.

5. You can't accuse them of stinting on the condiments – every table is generously stuffed with everything you might need.

Fancy roof terrace.

NOTICE
VEHICLES AND CONTENTS ARE LEFT HERE ENTIRELY AT OWNERS RISK

PJ'S TRANSPORT CAFE / DRAYCOTT-IN-THE-CLAY, STAFFORSHIRE

PJ's is a fantastic working cafe just off the A50, on the road to Litchfield. It's not fancy or a design classic or anything. It's not swimming in acres of faded formica and if they go out of business no-one's going to be running to the papers blaming Starbucks. It's just a great, basic cafe; a triumph of British cafe culture. Cheap, decent food, Utility surroundings. Somewhere for a working person to rest and watch Sky before getting back into the cab.

1. When will English Heritage start lobbying to preserve fluorescent signs?

2. Huge, pale, piping hot chips. An egg with a similarly pale vibe. And lovely dark bacon hinting at the less utilised bits of the pig. A brilliant fry-up. And delivered at top speed too.

3. Looking at this picture again I remember really enjoying this cup of tea. I'd just given up having sugar in my tea and I was really feeling the loss of it. I was starting to think that what I'd spent my whole life thinking was a deep love of tea was in fact a deep love of sugar. But this cup of tea put me back on the right path. This was one of those industrial strength cups of tea that only a good transport cafe can do – so thick and strong it's chewable, and I could really taste and appreciate the tea. God bless you PJ's.

Note the lone pea

THE SALT BOX / HATTON (A511), DERBYSHIRE

The Salt Box is a great transport cafe. Which proudly boasts of real chips. Real, delicious chips. And thick, pink bacon. And incredibly hot tea.

1. There's nothing quaint or retro about it. It's a bit like someone's conservatory, but it's a fantastically efficient place for serving large quantities of delicious fried food.

2. The Salt Box is a local institution and landmark. They've even got a certificate boasting of their visit from the Bishop of Derby.

1. The trucks gathered in the car park have that stirring look of *Convoy* about them. I bet there's a Norbert Dentressangle in there somewhere.

OP! YE MAY GANG FAUR AND FARE WAUR

STRACATHRO SERVICES / (A90) NORTH OF BRECHIN

This place is absolutely superb. A glorious stop on a splendid road, very generously equipped with great cafes. I presume the sign means 'you could go a long way and do worse'. I like that sentiment. Modest and persuasive at the same time.

1. They deal with a demanding audience of truckers, so as you'd expect, the EBC&B is magnificent. Generous portions. Speedy cooking. Lovely taste. I especially like that mottled texture on the egg.

2. Simple condiment configuration. You don't see so many of this kind of salt/pepper things these days. I wonder why not.

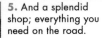

5. And a splendid shop; everything you need on the road.

4. I presume these were flagpoles once. We should get a collection together to put some flags back up. How cheering would that be?

3. The inside of the place is brilliant. Simple and clean. With big windows and lights like my mum and dad used to have in their living room.

6. Look: a choice of soup. There's a lot of fancy restaurants that don't offer you a choice of soup.

THE BUS / THE LAY-BY (A52) BETWEEN DERBY AND ASHBOURNE

The Bus is an exception that proves a rule. Or something. They don't do chips, so technically they shouldn't be in here, but it's such a great cafe that I felt you should know about it. It's run by Arthur and Rita who seem to be friends with everyone, constantly harassed by their hundreds of customers and always on the verge of falling out – though they never do.

2. They've even got their own website. www.thebuscafe.com.

1. Doing chips would be hard on a bus, but they do a splendid job with everything else. Lovely dark bacon, nice rounded eggs, deeply orange beans. And it's always dead cheap, never the same price twice, but always very cheap.

3. Basic, comprehensive condiments, but more impressively, you're right next to a field. Yes, you're in a lay-by, but you're looking out a lovely rural scene.

This place is normally packed, especially on Saturday mornings, but Arthur and Rita seem to know everyone's name, and their order. This is a fantastic place.

WATLING STREET CAFE / JUNCTION 9, M1

Watling Street was built by the Romans as part of their occupation of Britain. The Watling Street Truck Stop cafe probably came a little later, but it's a significant contribution to world civilisation. The perfect place to break your M1 journey and stuff your face with tasty food.

1. The grub is magnificent – look at that – huge piles of gorgeousness. Delicious plump chips, pinky pinky bacon, beany beans and an eggy egg. And that fabulous promotional mug just sets it off a treat.

2. A basic set-up, everything else is done with sachets. Nice and economical. They have a simple ordering system here, you go up to the counter, place your order, pay and give your name, then take your seat. Later on they holler your name out and you collect your grub. The name they hollered just after mine was 'Fat Bastard'. I like that. You don't get that at Gary Rhodes' place.

3. The thing I especially like is they make a bit of an effort inside. Nice curtains. A telly. Some papers lying about. Truckers are a discriminating audience, they won't take any nonsense.

This establishment is patrolled by highly-trained guard cows. Can you see one hiding in this picture?

THE HORN / (A90) BETWEEN DUNDEE AND PERTH

The Horn is such a fantastic place and landmark that it gets its own brown sign on the A90. What an exceptional tribute. And well deserved.

Its first great claim to fame is it's got a cow on the roof. Seems simple when you state it like that but, trust me, it's quite striking as you beetle up the A90. Then, as you swing into the car-park you notice the second great claim to fame, which is more subtle and more lovely, which is that it's round. A perfect, curvaceous, 60s-feeling round. That starts you smiling as you park the car and you keep smiling until you're back on the road again.

1. The EBC&B makes you smile to start with. Lots of food crammed onto a smallish plate which makes it feel all the more bountiful. I thought the chips were especially straight but it's possible that writing this book has made me hypersensitive to chip linearity. Great contrast between a very pale egg and HUGE quantities of dark, curly bacon.

2. Minimal tableside condiment apportionment. But acceptably minimal.

3. One thing I love about a cafe is a system. A unique and individual way of getting food to you. And The Horn has a system. You start off by filing around a little serve yourself area – perhaps something tasty from one of these cases. Then you get your order in for your substantial fry-up and your warming beverage.

4. Clutching your strangely out of focus order and your large cow-themed number. See how the numbers correlate – they have a system.

5. The interior keeps you smiling too – because although round's a pretty impractical shape for a cafe it does allow for one big room – which means you can observe your fellow patrons with ease. And that's half the fun of a cafe.

6. And then, as your smile starts to fade as your mind considers the dangers of driving on an overful stomach you pass through the excellent gift-shop and you start grinning all over again. Everything you need to remember a Scottish holiday; slightly offensive car stickers and lots of shortbread.

OH I DO LIKE TO BE...

YOU DON'T HEAR much about the sea in modern Britain. You hear about inner cities and urban development and countryside alliances. But you don't hear about the sea. We haven't had a decent cod war for ages and tankers don't seem to dump oil into the sea with the same regularity they used to.

And you definitely don't hear about 'sea-faring'. When was the last time you heard Britain described as a sea-faring nation? We're not, we're a commuting nation.

The sea isn't part of modern life. We fly over it, we don't sail on it much. We don't make a living from it. We don't do paintings of it. And we don't worry about it as a bulwark of national defence. Do you see what I'm getting at? It feels like we don't think about the sea much these days.

Though we still like to be beside the seaside. We still like to be beside the sea.

... The pull of the bucket and spade, the sand and the shingle, the fish and the chip. Maybe it's the last vestige of our sea-faring heritage; our desire to get on a pedallo and drift aimlessly out to sea until the RNLI pluck our bodies, beetroot with exposure, from the middle of the Atlantic.

And for me, naturally, a huge part of the seaside experience is the seaside cafe. The temple of ice-cream and salt, Horlicks and hygienic hard-wood chip forks.

Some things to think about seaside cafes:

1. They don't all do the EBC&B

The twin drivers of the seaside culinary economy are ice-cream and chips. They keep the seaside communities going, and it has to be faced, you don't always fancy a fry-up at the seaside. It might be too hot. Or you might want a knickerbocker glory. Or you might find a bit of bacon reminds you too much of your own skin after you fell asleep and the sun came out unexpectedly.

But sometimes, just sometimes, the ebcb is exactly what you're after. Maybe you're enjoying a cold Easter break in Skegness; it's been raining for three days and the kids have exploited all the possibilities of the arcades, you've read every Robert Ludlum for miles around and you've no idea what to do next.

2. They sell everything

Sunglasses, rock, buckets, spade, little flags, toy cars, replica trawlers, chocolate, fishing nets, ice-cream, newspapers, Robert Ludlum books, hats, visors, wrist bands, towels, beach bags, plasters, RNLI tea towels, rubber spiders, big things made from shells, little things made from shells, other things made from shells, sun-cream, umbrellas, aspirin, anoraks, toy soldiers, wooden spoons featuring local scenes, disposable cameras, egg, bacon, chips and beans.

3. They're always trying to get you outside

Seaside cafes are always in denial about the real seaside experience (rain, misery, tea) so they're always trying to create a Riviera experience, which normally means plastic garden furniture on the pavement next to the car park across from the shopping arcade which is right next to the sea. So you sit out there unsure whether you're going to be squinting at the sun or sheltering from the rain. You feel like you'd maybe like to go inside but you think you'd be letting them down if you do that. Almost admitting that Camber is not Cannes and Newbiggen is not Nice. And you wouldn't want to do that.

4. They open when they want to

Seaside opening hours are, to say the least, variable.

To start with you have to deal with the fact that the British seaside has a fragile economy, balanced between our weather and Easyjet prices to somewhere warm. So most cafe-workers have at least a couple of jobs and since they only get busy when the tourists arrive they're often somewhere else when you're battering at the door, pointing at your watch.

And then you add that indefinable sense of seaside-time; that sense that whether you're in Bondi or Bournemouth, seaside places operate with a sort of relaxed hippy sloth. It seems that there's some mysterious connection with the ocean that makes seaside people slightly indolent (by inland standards). Ancient landladies or pierced students, they all have that faintly leathery skin, that mad-staring gaze and that tendency to take forever with your cappuccino.

And that's what makes a seaside cafe one of the best places in the world.

WITH
REAL
FRUIT
JUICE!

SOLD HERE!

BESIDE THE SEASIDE

6

KIT KAT CAFE / OLD LYDD ROAD, CAMBER SANDS, EAST SUSSEX

The Kit Kat is the perfect beach cafe; right on the sand, they sell everything, they do a great fry-up and they're lovely people. Camber is a fascinating place, it's a huge, beautiful beach really close to London. By rights it should be the Hamptons of London. Lots of huge expensive seafront properties owned by the very glamorous, and all sorts of expensive restaurants and boutiques. But it's not like that; because it's surrounded by a nuclear power station, all sorts of mysterious military installations and a housing estate which has a distinct occupied territories feel. This keeps Camber fairly authentic, by which of course I mean, cheap. And it means great cafes are doing good business serving ordinary people proper food. None of that Rick Thingy seabass here.

1. Of course being British I sit inside when I can; you don't want to risk getting any sun. But if you're adventurous you can grab yourself a chair and a cup of tea and keep a close eye on your children playing merrily by the sea (which seems to be about a mile away when the tide's out). or bouncing like lunatics on the nearby trampolines. I think this is the moment when a child's head has hit the sand with a sickening thud.

2. They do a munificent EBC&B, which seems to come with double egg as standard. And what big, delicious golden eggs; like fluffy beds of protein. And the chips are piled on with a casual flair that might appeal to an avant-garde florist. Deep pink bacon, generous beans. And a very good cup of tea. The tea has all that specialness of tea on the beach but with none of the metallic tang from your Mum's knackered vacuum flask.

3. I love these things; the things you get so they can find you with your order. Presumably they're visible over more of the beach than those little white triangles you sometimes get.

4. Beach cafes are often feverish hives of entrepreneurialism, they have to get as much money as they can out of a limited season, so they sell anything and everything.

5. A very simple condiment set-up; the sauce comes in sachets. That makes sense at the beach, you can imagine sauce dispensers and sand don't mix well.

Poor old Herne Bay pier

café

SEAVIEW CAFE / TANKERTON SLOPES, WHITSTABLE, KENT

The Seaview Cafe is located on the long, slow sweep of road which takes you from Whitstable to Herne Bay along the seafront. It's a brilliant cafe and always busy. The food's good and the people seem friendly enough, although they're always working flat out (especially at the weekend). We visited this cafe on the weekend of the Whitstable regatta which was great because all sorts of big, fat, slow boats ambled past during the course of our meal. It's got writing on the roof, (presumably to taunt starving pilots in light aircraft) and you can just about make out the end of Herne Bay pier in the distance, now a forlorn island since the pier dropped into the sea some years ago.

Another guest contribution. This bit of writing and these pictures from Tony Lyons, gentleman and designer of this book.

1. Look at that for a view. The odd-looking boat is called an oyster yawl.

2. And look at this for a previously unencountered eccentricity: a table mat featuring a decent pen and ink rendering of the exterior of the cafe.

3. A good condiment selection: charming earthenware salt and pepper pots, the standard HP and a cunning twist on the whole thing provided by the Sainsbury's ketchup. The kids rated it, so who am I to grumble?

4. New to the EBC&B game as I am, I was really impressed with this. The chips were crisp and as hot as lava, the beans had a good juice to bean ratio, the bacon was pleasingly salty with a hint of burnt at the edge and the egg had had fat flicked over the top to eliminate any trace of raw albumen. Top drawer.

TOWER RESTAURANT / 107 LUMLEY ROAD, SKEGNESS

The Tower is one of those huge places you only get at the seaside – designed to extract maximum custom from rainy days and a short summer. It's on the main drag in Skeggy – honoured seaside town of childhood. (If you're from Derby you have to go to Skegness for your holidays.) And it's just across from the Aroma Coffee Bar – also worth a visit.

1. The EBC&B is superb – complemented by the quality crockery you get at the Tower. The very generous bean allocation masks some gorgeous seaside chips and nice pink bacon. And look at that funny egg – it looks a little like an alien seed-pod has popped out just a few seconds earlier.

2. Pay your bill or be cursed by The Eagle of The Tower.

3. They've gone for that rustic / slightly ski-lodge feeling. Lots of wood and candle-like lights. But they've gone a bit further than most would – with antlers and stuffed birds scattered around the place. And it's huge – seating for 160. Imagine 160 people chomping down on knickerbocker glories and banana splits. That's the glory of the seaside.

GENTS

4. Gents is the perfect cafe word. 'Gentlemen' is too formal, too posh. 'Men' is too unfriendly and matter of fact. But 'Gents' is just right. The right mix of friendliness and respect.

BROWN LIQUIDS

THE EBC&B IS incomplete without a hot beverage, or, more specifically, a brown liquid. I've never really understood that. Why are all our fry-up accompaniments brown? Tea. Coffee. Horlicks. Bovril. Ovaltine. All brown. Odd that.

Tea vs. Coffee

The big two are obviously tea and coffee. I'm a 90% tea man. I have to be jolted out of my routine to have a coffee. The Camp Coffee at the New Piccadilly'll do it. Or the possibility of doing a 50s throwback frothy coffee in those lovely brown transparent cups and saucers. But most of the time I'm all about the tea. And most people are like that. They're either a tea person or a coffee person. It's one of those eternal divides, like cats or dogs, Bing or Frank, Socialist Workers' Party or Workers' Revolutionary Party.

The values and associations of each are quite clear. Coffee is energetic, foreign, modern and cool. It's about youth and rebellion for hundreds of years; from the first coffee houses acting as centres of radical thought and debate to Cliff and Tommy Steele meeting in Soho Coffee bars to organise the non-violent overthrow of squares through hip-gyrations and swearing.

Tea is different. Tea is slow, English, traditional, relaxing, reflective, quiet and frankly, a bit dull. You can see why I'm a tea man.

Plumbing

The mechanics of beverage production fascinate me. It's one of the first things you notice in a cafe; the vast assemblage of pipes and valves they use to deliver a semi-warm drink to your table. (Except on those occasions when they manage to invent a whole new state of matter; something that's still apparently a liquid but which has the brain-boiling properties of the gases on the surface of the sun.)

The glorious constructions of the coffee technicians have been much discussed elsewhere – the incredible

that steaming unleashing of tea. You get a taste from an urn which is quite different to the thin civilised texture of the domestic tea bag and kettle arrangement. Tea urn tea is thick, dark and meaty. You get the sense that there's something in that urn that dates back to the dawn of tea-history; that the urn contains some kind of uhr-tea which flavours every cup the cafe dishes out. The tea essence is like the yeast that brewers strive to preserve; giving the beer its essential quality. I like to imagine that if a cafe ever went up in flames (and it would probably be an insurance job) then the owner would dash back in for the urn. (And that, years later you'd still be able to taste some of the quality of that fire in the tea.)

Intellectuals and Brown Liquids

One of the great romances of the cafe is to sit and pretend to be intellectual. This requires a coffee. And ideally a cigarette, the stump of a pencil and a slim volume of poetry. Or something equally unreadable. You don't actually have to read it, you can read the cafe's copy of *The Mirror* if you like. But you've got to leave it somewhere conspicuous, in case a fellow intellectual wanders by and wants to start a conversation about the death of intimacy in working-class social spaces.

Coffee seems more suitable for intellectual work because it delivers more caffeine; more of a jolt to the brain. This gives you the sense that you're thinking harder and faster, your thoughts are racing and are therefore better. And since you've obviously been up all night thinking difficult thoughts you need a coffee to wake you up.

And coffee lets you ally yourself with various different schools of caffeinated thought:

1. The French Pretentionalists – the original espresso elite. Sartre. De Beauvoir. Street cafes. Rive Gauche. (The geographical feature not the perfume). Gauloises. Les Deux Maggots. Knowing laughter. Fierce denunciation. Raised eyebrows. Large bowls of coffee with delicious pastries. Early death.

2. The Beat Elite – the American world of java and jeans. Ginsberg. Kerouac. Pollock. Typewriters. Lucky strikes. Streams of consciousness. Paperbacks and firearms. Roadside diners. Black coffee and hoagies. Early death.

3. The Soho Miserablists – our home-grown bunch of cafe intellectuals. Farson. Barnard. Various Freuds. *Absolute Beginners*. Little cups of bad cappuccino and desultory plates of scampi. The Partisan Cafe. Collars turned against the rain. Woodbines. Penguin paperbacks. Demob suits and utility furniture. Jazz, Formica and bongos – all in black and white. Early death.

So grab an intellectual tradition, pop down to the bookshop, pick up a Penguin and get to the cafe for a quick four-hour coffee.

FUNCTIONAL FOOD

LET'S BE REALISTIC. We mostly eat food because we have to. It's primarily not an aesthetic experience, it's a functional one. We're eating for energy. And there's no more functional meal than egg, bacon, chips and beans. Lots of protein, lots of calories. It's gotten people through marathons, hangovers and extended night-time sorties over Berlin. And, time was, this view of food was Britain's gift to the world. Fancy food was something foreigners did, like art and sex and surrendering. We knew better. We weren't seduced by cookery books and fresh ingredients.

But not any more. Now every perfectly respectable inner-city NCP is desecrated with a Farmer's Market and school children are being deprived off their inalienable right to spend their dinner money on chips and curly-wurlys.

Instead we should celebrate our uniquely British perspective on food and foodery. What are the two great British gifts to food culture? Easy – imaginative uses of offal and food you can carry around. Now, it's not my place here today to talk about offal (though I'm from the East Midlands so I know a bit about it) but I would like to remind people of our noble cultures of portable food. Functional food at its finest.

Think about the Cornish pasty.

Why that peculiar shape? Why that strange pie?

For functional reasons of course.

It was designed so Cornish tin miners could stick their lunch in their pocket. Perfect. A delicious pastry case wrapped around some lovely spicy meaty stuff. And even more cleverly, that ridge along the back (which was originally much bigger, like the pointy bits of a stegosaurus) was designed so the miners could eat the pasty and then throw that bit away – that way they didn't have to touch any of the food they were actually going to eat with their tin-stained hands. Talk about biodegradable packaging. And so we get the Pork Pie and the Sausage Roll and the Scotch Egg. And the Kebab. And fish and chips. All designed to be edible on the move, without any of that sitting down, appreciating it nonsense.

And then there's the ultimate achievement in functional food technology. The sandwich. The genius

invention of one of our own noble peers. Not invented in order to advance culinary science or to uncover taste explosions or any Frenchified notions like that. No. It was invented so he could stuff his face while continuing to play cards.

Let's remember the Earl of Sandwich. Let's celebrate his genius and remember that food doesn't always have to be delicious, sometimes it just has to be convenient.

FREQUENTLY ASKED QUESTIONS

Since this thing began as a website I thought I'd do a quick FAQ to finally answer many of the questions I get online.

Doesn't eating all these fried meals make you fat? Aren't there health concerns?

Yes it does. I am fat. There are health concerns. Or there would be if this was all I ate. In fact, on average I only have a full EBC&B every other week. (Though averages lie. In making this book I did once have four in one day; what a day).

As you'll see if you look at the blog, I did once take a few months off to train for and run a 10K because I was worried about the fat. Now I'm trying to balance the two though; I figure that if I run 20k a week I'm also entitled to an EBC&B every week. And this plan is really working well at the moment, apart from the running.

What's your favourite cafe ever?

I'm not going to answer this on the grounds that it might incriminate me. How could I go into my regular cafes when they all might know that they're not my favourite? That wouldn't be right. And anyway I don't have a favourite. It's like asking a parent who their favourite child is. You can't answer it. You love them all for different reasons.

I will say this though – The Hatton Salt Box in Derbyshire does the best chips in the country.

Who does the best chips in the country?

You're just not listening are you?

Sorry. Er. How come so many of the cafes you review are in London or the East Midlands?

That's a better question with a slightly longer answer.

There's a lot in London for two reasons. Firstly, this is where I live and therefore mostly where I eat. So a lot of these places are regular haunts of mine. I'm in Sky 2 almost every day, and The Marketplace Cafe almost as often. I love these places. So they're going to be in the book.

Also, it has to be said, London has a very strong culture of interesting and quirky cafes. There's a huge density of really interesting places here; from classic mid-century places with the fascinating décor to some great 70s throwbacks to the really characterful working places of yesterday and today. If you want to fill your day with great cafes, you come to London.

Why the East Midlands? Partly convenience, partly regional pride. I'm from the East Midlands (Derby actually) and I go back up there a lot. We stay in a place between Ashbourne and Uttoxeter, near the JCB factory. It's more idyllic than it sounds. So we're often filling a wet weekend by visiting another cafe. And we've become very familiar with the transport cafes of the M1 and the A50.

But I'm also waging a small war for regional fairness. I'm convinced that the East Midlands doesn't get a fair shake within the national culture. When was the last time you heard an East Midlands accent on the telly? (I'll tell you when – when the beloved Brian Clough died. Then you heard the folk of Derby and Nottingham in full cry, but even Brian's unlikely to die twice, so I bet you don't hear them again for a while) Would you even recognise an East Midlands accent if you heard one?

So part of that war is an up-weighting of East Midlands cafes.

And part of it is a down-weighting of the most over-rated tourist-attraction unit in the whole country – the Lake District. Yes it's quite pretty, yes some writers hung out there once. But ask yourself, what has it done for you lately? It's all traffic jams and teashops, daffodils and whining. It gets on the telly a lot because the establishment all have third homes there, but it's not a patch on the Peak District. And that's why there are no Lake District cafes in here. (And it's nothing to do with laziness or not ever finding anywhere I liked.)

What was that film with that cafe in? That one with that bloke in it?

You may well be thinking of *Quadrophenia*. That's got good cafe scenes in it.

Or there's the fantastic Refreshment Room at Milford Junction in *Brief Encounter* or the Kardomah, where Celia Johnson and Trevor Howard meet for lunch. The best thing about that place is that it's absolutely stinking thick with cigarette smoke and yet if you look at the back wall of the restaurant there's a big sign pointing down some stairs saying 'Smoking Room' – if it's this smoky in the rest of the place what must the Smoking Room be like? You could probably hang on the smoke in there, or walk on it, or use it to insulate your wall cavities.

Or there's a good cabbies' cafe in *Adventures Of A Taxi Driver*, one of those 70s British sex comedies with no sex and lots of people who used to be in *On The Buses*.

Or there's Michael Caine's version of *Alfie*. He picks up a 'bird' in a magnificent place called the Busy Bee, with a jukebox and a pinball machine and lovely curtains.

Or there's the magnificent Stanley Baker in *Hell Drivers*; a gritty, bitter tale of British lorry drivers, racing round the countryside in horribly unconvincing 'fast motion'. Clashes of manly egos and driving skills all come to a head in a marvellously grim transport cafe where the relentless theme is miserable utility. You'd just love to be the nervous family gathered at the back of the cafe when they all get into a fight. The food looks to be industrial in quality and quantity.

But for me, you can't beat a tiny moment in the splendid Scottish film *Gregory's Girl*. Remember that? John Gordon Sinclair and a cameo from Claire Grogan? There's a scene of perfect delicacy set in a shopping centre Wimpy Bar; between John Gordon Sinclair's character (a lovelorn teenager) and his little sister (wise before her years). It's full of teenage wistfulness about the British suburbs ('this isn't Italy. No style') and the sad content of childhood. ('What do you dream about?' 'Just ginger beer and ice cream. I'm still a little girl, remember?'). And then she sums up the cafe experience in one tiny, lovely thought. 'The nicest part is just before you taste it.'

So what's the appeal of these places anyway?

Well, that's the biggy isn't it?
There's a few things:
I like the variety of people you get in a good cafe. They attract all kinds of everyone. Working people filling up. Intellectuals being classless. The posh recovering from hangovers.

I like the people who own them. It takes energy and ingenuity to keep a modern cafe going. It's not easy, and it takes interesting people. And the people who run cafes are the best argument in the world for unrestricted immigration. Cafe culture was built by immigrants and they're the people who are keeping it going. It used to be the Italians; now it's the Estonians, the Polish, the Thai, it's everyone. They're the people who are willing to do the hours, scrape by on the money and put up with the drunks because they know that however rough it is owning a cafe it's a solid business. People will always want fried food.

I like the anonymity. You can pop into a cafe, order without making eye contact with anyone, and leave without exchanging a word. You can be lost in your thoughts or hidden behind your paper. You're in the cafe, but you're in your own little world.

I like the artificial nostalgia. There's a weird phenomenon in the modern world, that increasing nostalgia many of us feel for something we don't remember in the first place. Steam trains, Routemasters, *Brief Encounter*, Bovril at football matches, Pez dispensers, we think of these things fondly even if we don't remember them. Many cafes evoke this sense very powerfully.

I like the randomness. On the surface, cafes are entirely predictable. There's a limited number of chair, table, counter, condiment configurations. The food tends to be in the same culinary ballpark, there's rarely performance art or a string quartet to surprise you. But there's still all this randomness and unpredictability. Cafe owners are masters of their own little domains and they exercise all their rights with considerable abandon. Just look at the art they put on the walls. It's art you've never seen anywhere else, art you can't begin to understand, art you can't help staring at.

I like being out of the house. Not because being in the house is bad but because leaving the house gives you a small sense of achievement. In *Seinfeld*, George explains why he wants to watch a video at Jerry's place rather than at home; 'Because if I watch (a video) at my apartment I feel like I'm not doing anything. If I watch it here, I'm out of the house; I'm doing something.' Cafes do the same thing. You have a cup of coffee at home you're an idler, you have one in a cafe you might be a revolutionary poet.

I like the food. I like egg, bacon, chips and beans.

ALL THE LADIES IN THE HOUSE SAY EBC&B

Author's note: My wife kept telling me I should write a piece about the experience of being a woman in a cafe. But I couldn't do it. So I asked her to. And here it is. Anne, take it away:

ONCE UPON A time there was a lady. One day, she was going about her usual tasks and quests and so forth when suddenly she realised that she was hungry. In the distance, she noticed a long line of men, following each other, one after another, into a small, welcoming building. From the open door into which the men were trooping, a delicious aroma glided towards our heroine. Filled with excitement and hunger, she hurried to follow the gorgeous smell. But alas, when she reached the door, the kindly Inn Keeper regarded her with a strange, unknowing look.

'I'm sorry,' he said, 'but what are you? I don't recognise your form.'

'I'm a single lady, wanting to eat double egg and chips alone in your cafe?' she replied.

The Inn Keeper smiled and said, 'Sorry love, but I don't understand what you're saying.'

OK, enough with the fairy tale. It's not quite that bad, but for a single gal, the world of the cafe is one of the last great unknowns. It's just not something you see very much, ladies sitting alone in cafes eating the kind of food celebrated in this book. Why? Why is it that the cafe – the kind of cafe which has never seen a sun dried tomato or heard of mozzarella – remains an almost wholly male place?

I'm married to the author of this book so I've been in a fair few cafes in my time, eaten any number of egg, beans and chips. Of course, I do see other women in there but not many. Why?

Here's one answer. It's a speed thing. Cafes don't necessarily encourage lingering so women worry that there won't be enough time to chat, to tease apart the details of each other's lives. However, as most men I know live in fear of prolonged social intimacy, this limited window is a huge boon for them.

Also I think many women just don't want to be seen in public eating the kind of food which makes the cafe worthwhile. In the privacy of our own homes, we're happy to shove down half a packet of chocolate hobnobs, but woe betide any lady seen eating a fried egg (two and a half points) in a public setting.

It's a shame though. Single women in cafes are treated terribly well. If you're a woman in a cafe on your own, people are nice to you. The staff call you 'darling' and 'luv' and 'duck' and it doesn't sound horrid and sexist because usually the person serving you is a lovely woman just like yourself. Well, maybe more like your mother or teenage daughter, but like you have been or will be. They take extra care of you. Even the men. Particularly the men. The builders and traffic wardens, the lorry drivers and sales reps, they will tone down their language because a single lady is present. It's charming, really.

And without wanting to suggest that women and children have to be lumped together, cafes are generally a good bet for families. There's stuff on the menu that children will actually eat and it doesn't have to be chips. It is impossible to discuss something so quintessentially English as the cafe without mentioning class. So, cards on the table, my roots are lower middle class. We never went into cafes with my parents but then we never ate out with my parents full stop, except for the occasional seaside fish and chips while on camping holidays in various bleak and inhospitable coastal resorts. My parents would still never dream of going into a cafe, except when they are with us, when they're terribly thrilled by the experience. These days I'm definitely middle-middle class, if such a thing exists. I know that, if I'm honest, cafes make me feel as if I'm going back to some kind of working class roots which I never had in the first place. I tell myself that if I take my son in often enough it will act as a balance for all the times we go to Yo! Sushi, his favourite restaurant, and, that Mecca for all middle class families, Pizza Express. And, to some extent, it does. He sees people in cafes who do real jobs, builders who make things, police who protect our streets, men and women who drive stuff up and down the country. Nearly everyone we know does something in an office, something involving much email and measurable outputs – and they have a Prêt a Manger sandwich for lunch. At least the cafe provides a different view of the world, albeit no more or less authentic.

So, imagine our heroine has made it to her table and is sitting with her egg and chips before her, a mug of steaming tea in her hand. She's alone but happy enough to be Johnny no-mates. Not having to talk is a relief really. Twenty minutes of just being herself.

And that's all before she puts the first chip in her mouth.

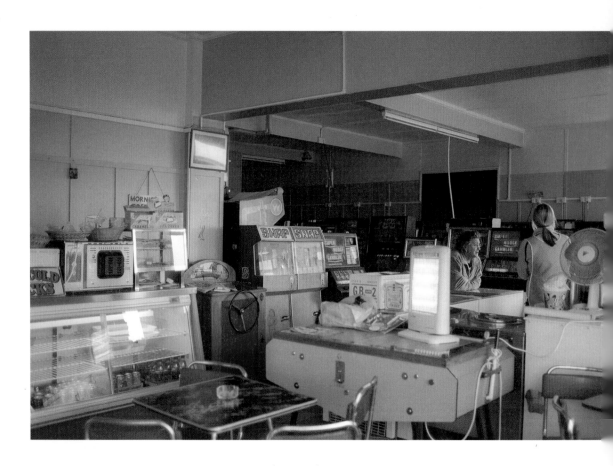

LOOKING BACK IT'S SO BIZARRE

WHEN I WAS at school I never imagined I'd write a book. Particularly one about fried food and cafes. Especially one that quoted Level 42 lyrics in the chapter headings. And yet I just have. And this is the last bit, the bit where I wrap everything up in nice concluding thoughts and send you to bed thinking happy thoughts, resolving to eat more fried food (and hopefully to do more exercise to compensate).

So what have I learned?

1. Cafes are great because they change, not because they stay the same.
There's nothing like the pleasure of an old fifties throwback cafe; the Formica, the brown glass coffee cups, the decrepitude, the peeling air of miserabalism. I love those places. But I know their end is inevitable, because that's part of their charm. We can, and should, preserve many of the fixtures and the fittings but we can't preserve the atmosphere because a great cafe is also a great business, not a museum, and great businesses change and move on and evolve. Great cafes die every week, it's a huge shame, but it's the reality of small business life. And you can't blame people like Starbucks, it's not their fault, they're not really even in the same business. But for every great cafe that dies, a new one is born. And realising that, and discovering the new ones, is one of life's huge pleasures. And, of course, the best cafes just go on and on, updating themselves just enough, adding new little ideas on top of the old ones, accruing layers of change which create their uniqueness. And that's lovely.

2. Great British cafes depend upon a regular flow of the Non-British.
Cafes are built on immigration. Enterprising foreigners are often the only people willing to do the hours and they're often the customers too. Especially at 6 in the morning. Cafe cultures are built on their labour and their love and cafe food is built from the melding of our traditional stodge with their imported cuisine. Once it was the Greeks and Italians, now it's people from Eastern Europe, from Thailand, from everywhere. These are the people who'll preserve the great British cafe.

3. Writing in numbered points is much easier than trying to sustain any kind of logical narrative thrust using paragraphs and that.
I'm surprised Dickens didn't work that out.

4. Fry-ups are delicious.
I know it's pathetic but after all this thinking and writing that's the best I can come up with. They're just delicious. They fill you up, cheer you up and make you feel like life's worth living. We should all spend more time in cafes, eating fry-ups.